Shadow

Copyright © 2021 as a collection, Damien Freeman; individual chapters, the contributors.

ALL RIGHTS RESERVED. This book contains material protected under International and Federal Copyright Laws and Treaties. Any unauthorised reprint or use of this material is prohibited. No part of this book may be reproduced or transmitted in any form or by any means, electronic or mechanical, including photocopying, recording, or by any information storage and retrieval system without express written permission from the publisher.

Published by Connor Court Publishing under the imprint The Kapunda Press. The Kapunda Press is an imprint of Connor Court Publishing in association with the PM Glynn Institute, Australian Catholic University.

CONNOR COURT PUBLISHING PTY LTD

PO Box 7257
Redland Bay QLD 4165
sales@connorcourt.com www.connorcourt.com

Cover picture: Elric Ringstad, *Blue Sky Power* (c.2019), oil, bees wax, damar on canvas

ISBN: 9781922449740 (pbk.)

Cover design by Ian James

—SHADOW— OF THE CROSS

Catholic Social Teaching & Australian Politics

GREG CRAVEN

"The whole modern world has divided itself into Conservatives and Progressives. The business of Progressives is to go on making mistakes. The business of the Conservatives is to prevent the mistakes from being corrected."

                    G. K. Chesterton

Contents

Foreword
Zlatko Skrbiš ix

Introduction
Damien Freeman 1

Catholic teaching and Australian politics

Australian political problems and Catholic policy solutions
Greg Craven 13

Responding to Greg Craven

1. Teaching for best selves not best governments
Tony Abbott 59

2. Opening dialogue in government, education and workplace
Philip Booth 67

3. Beyond principles alone
Sandie Cornish 81

4. Continuing impact on a changing political agenda
Kevin Rudd 99

Epilogue
Frank Brennan 111

Contributors 125
Notes 127
Index 137

Foreword

Zlatko Skrbiš

CATHOLIC SOCIAL TEACHING represents the magisterium of the Catholic Church on issues of social importance. At its heart is the belief that a just society is one in which all people have absolute value and are afforded consideration and respect. As such, the recurring themes in Catholic social teaching, such as human dignity, the common good, subsidiarity, and solidarity hold an important place in political conversation. This is because the values which are espoused place people before partisanship.

This book engages in a thoughtful discussion on the relevance of Catholic social teaching in Australian politics. My predecessor Professor Greg Craven AO leads the conversation by arguing that Catholic social teaching is a resource that can help shape Australian public policy. Respondents to his essay, including eminent scholars and former Australian prime ministers, each offer their own distinctive perspective on the proposition.

What is important about this book is that it contributes to the broader dialogue pertaining to how the interests of all

Australians can be best served and respected. It also revisits the issue of how religion might make a meaningful contribution to public policy in contemporary Australian society. Many of us have long cherished the legacy of Catholic social teaching and so this is a dialogue which I truly hope others will be inspired to engage in—regardless of their religious or political viewpoint.

Professor Zlatko Skrbiš
Vice-Chancellor and President
Australian Catholic University

Introduction

Damien Freeman

Sir Gerard Brennan retired as Chief Justice of Australia in 1998 and spent a small part of his retirement teaching a seminar on the High Court of Australia with Professor George Winterton at the University of New South Wales. I obtained permission from the University of Sydney to attend this seminar as part of my studies, and this proved to be one of the decisive moments of my life. I cannot remember what we were discussing, but someone said something that prompted Professor Winterton to remark in passing, "And then, of course, there are those who take a perverse pleasure in being gratuitously archaic—like Justice Meagher." And it came to pass that I had my great moment of self-realisation—that I too was one of the people who shared this perverse pleasure, and my life's course was set.

When Mr Justice Meagher retired from the Court of Appeal, the Chief Justice of New South Wales told him, "I am confident you will, one day, find your Boswell." In this I heard my calling to play Boswell to his Johnson, and I went on to write a book about him. In *Roddy's Folly*, I quoted one of his gratuitously archaic remarks about Sir Gerard's son: "Father Frank Brennan is the archetype of the modern Jesuit: short on Greek verbs, long on witchetty grubs." I still enjoy the humour in this quip and lament the shortage of Greek verbs in our life in common. Criticism of my book led me to reflect, however, on Justice Meagher's witchetty grubs, and on my rashness in dismissing out of hand something profound in Father Brennan's concern for the plight of Aboriginal people. He and I have not seen eye-to-eye on matters relating to Indigenous affairs in the years that have passed since then, but I, at least, came to see that he was right to advocate strenuously for something that I had all too readily dismissed out of hand.

What was it that led him and his modern Jesuits to see the profound challenges for Australia where Roddy Meagher and I could see only the witchetty grubs? A clue, perhaps, came to light whilst researching *Roddy's Folly*, when I came across a letter that Roddy's aunt, Mother Ellen Meagher, wrote to him. She had began her religious life at the Convent of the Sacred Heart in Rose Bay and ended it as a missionary in Japan. She was writing to him on the occasion of his father's death. In offering him her condolences, she reflected on her memories of the childhood she shared with his father, and remarked in passing of "our happy home life which was, however, overshadowed by the Cross."

It occurred to me that just as the story of Jesus' passion, which is embodied in the symbol of the Cross, might form the narrative that backgrounds the flourishing domestic life of a family, something derived from it might also form the background for the flourishing life in common of a political entity, such as a nation state. This, I have come to see, is indeed what Catholic social teaching aspires to be. As my colleague at Australian Catholic University, Peta Goldburg, explains, Catholic social teaching undoubtedly "provides a set of key principles and guidelines for action which can be used to evaluate situations, policies, and approaches used in contemporary society and offers valuable insights regarding the intersection between faith, society, and politics." In doing so, it has "drawn criticism from some politicians, journalists, and theologians who insist that the Church should not interfere in secular matters." This is despite the fact that, at the Second Vatican Council, the Catholic Church asserted "the right and duty of the Church to comment on worldly affairs because it is essentially concerned with the spiritual and material wellbeing of all people." She explains that, for over a century, the church has "critiqued society and offered advice about social and economic structures without aligning with any specific political party or ideological movement."[1]

Goldburg's suggestion that Catholic social teaching "challenges people to develop an authentic faith-based response to changing social, political, cultural, and economic conditions" is not particularly controversial. It naturally leads to recognition of the central place of such teaching in education. As recently as 2017, the Congregation for Catholic Education emphasised the significance of Catholic social teaching for education:

> Education to fraternal humanism must make sure that learning knowledge means becoming aware of an ethical universe in which the person acts. In particular, this correct notion of the ethical universe must open up progressively wider horizons of the common good, so as to embrace the entire human family ... the specific task that education to fraternal humanism can perform is to contribute to building such a culture based on intergenerational ethics.[2]

Things get more difficult, however, when the move is made from the formation of citizens who will participate in societies and economies to the formation of those societies and economies. Perhaps, there is a place for Catholic social teaching in the development and critique of societies and economies. Certainly, the case can be made that it has had some formative influence on these in Australia. Yet, even accepting that it can have a legitimate influence, things become trickier when it comes to the development of specific social and economic policies. Can Catholic social teaching not only serve as a broad formative influence on secular Australian society, but as a resource for the development of specific public policies? Greg Craven is representative of those who answer this question in the affirmative. He maintains that it is not merely a position from which to critique politics, but a resource to be drawn upon when developing specific public policies.

Greg Craven was born in Melbourne in 1958 and educated at St Kevin's College and the University of Melbourne, from which he graduated with a bachelor's degree in arts and a master's degree in law. From 2008 until 2020, he served as the third vice-chancellor of Australian Catholic University, having previously held executive positions at Curtin University of Technology and the University of Notre Dame Australia. His academic career began at the University of Melbourne in 1982, where he was successively a tutor, lecturer, and reader, before being appointed foundation dean and professor of law at Notre Dame in 1997, after having served as Crown Counsel in the Victorian Attorney-General's Department between 1992 and 1995. He has also been a member of numerous government advisory committees on matters including prostitution, the legal profession, law reform, federation, teacher education, and tertiary education quality and standards. His publications include *Secession* (1986), *The Convention Debates* (1987), *Australian Federation* (1991), *Future Proofing Australia* (2013) and, with Frank Brennan and Michael Casey, *Chalice of Liberty* (2018). In 2004, he was awarded the West Australian Premier's Book Award for Non-Fiction for his *Conversations with the Constitution*. He has been fêted by sovereigns, having been awarded the Centenary Medal and appointed an Officer of the Order of Australia, a Knight of the Equestrian Order of the Holy Sepulchre, a Knight of Magistral Grace of the Order of St John of Jerusalem, and a Knight Grand Cross of the Order of St Gregory the Great, yet remains an ardent republican.

In 2016, Craven established the Patrick McMahon Glynn Institute as Australian Catholic University's public policy think-tank. Shortly thereafter, its foundation director, Michael Casey, developed the PM Glynn Monograph Series, which, he explains, is "a series of short studies of some of the major strands of political philosophy in Australia and how they inform the practice of politics." Three books have been commissioned as part of this series. The first was published by Melbourne University Press; the second and third by the Kapunda Press, the Institute's imprint. I was commissioned to write about conservatism in 2016, and I published *Abbott's Right: the conservative tradition from Menzies to Abbott* in 2017. Adrian Pabst was commissioned to write about social democracy in 2018, and he published *Story of Our Country: Labor's vision for Australia* in 2019. Finally, Tim Wilson was commissioned in 2019 to write about liberalism, and he published *The New Social Contract: renewing the liberal vision for Australia* in 2020.

Abbott's Right begins with a discussion of the values of the Australian people and the way that leaders of the federal Liberal Party of Australia have articulated the fit between their own values and those of the people they govern by balancing liberal and conservative aspects of Australian society. It then offers an account of the conservative approach to public policymaking as a *cast of mind* rather than as an ideology; a middle way between pragmatism and theorising that regards the values of the tradition as a guide for progress. This is the approach first espoused by Edmund Burke and, *Abbott's Right* suggests, can be seen as underpinning the policymaking of Tony Abbott.

Story of Our Country begins with an assessment of when the Australian Labor Party has had most electoral success—and least success—and suggests such success can be seen when the party remains true to both its 'radical' and 'small-c conservative' character—a fused character that distinguishes it from other centre-left parties. Pabst then reflects on the legacy of Edmund Burke and Christian social teaching for the party; how these shaped the party's ethical outlook, and their implications for tensions between conservatives and progressives within the party. Such ideas are shown to be central to the party's understanding of the economic justice and social stability that enable people to pursue a good life. It is by developing policies shaped by this framework, He maintains, that Labor delivers on the promise of a "share in those things that make life worth living."

Introduction

The New Social Contract begins by defining classical liberalism as a belief in limited government and the freedom of individuals to choose how they live and to accept responsibility for their choices. A peculiarly Australian variant of liberalism is identified as a quest for an environment in which the equality and dignity of the individual is respected alongside the freedom to take responsibility for the individual's life and enterprise and the necessity of justice. It then considers the way in which liberalism became preoccupied with the *freedom* of the individual over the last thirty years at the expense of *empowerment* of the individual. In order for liberalism to maintain its electoral appeal, it is argued that liberals need to reaffirm their commitment to empowerment of the individual. A liberal programme for empowering the individual, Wilson maintains, will result in a new Australian social contract centred on liberalism.

On one level, Craven's essay in this volume offers a critique of the analyses offered by Pabst, Wilson, and me. On another level, it offers an alternative to them. Craven's alternative speaks to his fundamental criticism of all three approaches. Whatever the specific problems that their various arguments encounter, Craven maintains that they share a more fundamental defect, and this is the reason that they are all inadequate as a foundation for public policymaking. In contrast, he believes that Catholic social teaching can provide the kind of foundation that is missing from conservatism, liberalism, and social democracy.

Craven begins by tracing the historical developments from the French Revolution onwards. This required the Catholic Church to adopt a new approach to the political ideologies of liberalism and socialism in the nineteenth century; ideologies that were appealing to increasing numbers of the faithful. Pope Leo XIII's 1891 encyclical, *Rerum novarum*, is identified as the beginning of this new approach, and four key ideas are attributed to it and the tradition of Catholic social teaching that emerged from it: the dignity of the human person, the common good, subsidiarity, and solidarity. These four ideas stand in creative tension with one another. Although they are intended to provide a comprehensive vision of how a society should be organized, they are also a basis for providing a critique of the three dominant approaches to public policymaking in Australia, and Craven uses them to evaluate the approaches in *Story of Our Country*, *The New Social Contract*, and *Abbott's Right*. Whatever specific weaknesses Craven identifies in each approach, he also concludes that they share a more fundamental problem. Each lacks the kind of cohesive framework of principles that is capable of providing answers to the fundamental questions in policymaking. This has the effect of allowing policymaking to become purely transactional. Such pragmatism disconnected from a concrete vision of society has, Craven maintains, plagued policymaking in Australia for the last thirty years. He concludes his essay by offering some suggestions for how policymaking anchored in the principles of Catholic social teaching might deliver better policy outcomes for Australia in relation to education, healthcare, aged care, and Indigenous affairs.

Craven's essay is published in this volume together with four essays in response to it.

Tony Abbott offers two lines of criticism of Craven's

approach. First, he maintains that the church's social teaching should be seen as a resource for the formation of a country's citizens, but not a resource for the formation of the country's public policies. Secondly, he believes that in emphasising the significance of classical Catholic social teaching, Craven fails to acknowledge that the church's teaching developed over the course of a century, and the authentic modern position is to be found in Pope John Paul II's *Centesimus annus*, which emphasises the importance of the free market for a just society.

Kevin Rudd is a bit more optimistic about the role that Catholic social teaching might play in the development of public policy. He does agree with Abbott, however, that Craven's focus on classical Catholic social teaching fails to acknowledge its genuine relevance for contemporary society. As such, Rudd maintains that Pope Francis's encyclical, *Laudato si'*, with its focus on environmental issues rather than on industrial relations, should be seen as the most important resource that Catholic social teaching has to offer for the challenges of contemporary public policymaking in Australia.

Sandie Cornish's critique is somewhat more nuanced. Abbott and Rudd might be seen to disagree with Craven about the particular principles that are most important. Abbott senses that Craven prefers principles supporting distributism over those supporting the free market; Rudd that Craven prioritises principles of industrial relations over principles of environmental sustainability. On Cornish's account, however, both of these critiques fail to grasp what really matters about Catholic social teaching. Both assume that it is concerned with 'perennial principles', so that what is contested is the identity of these principles. She argues, however, that this is to misunderstand Catholic social teaching. Such teaching, she explains, needs to be understood as an evolving tradition in which new insights may be gained inductively by responding to changing circumstances, rather than by recourse to perennial principles. The principles have a role to play, but it is not the central one that might be suggested by the approach of Craven, Abbott, and Rudd.

Philip Booth takes exception to Craven's treatment of liberalism (rather as Abbott takes exception to the treatment of conservatism), although he sees much of value in Craven's discussion of education. Booth, like Cornish, has something to say about the way in which Catholic social teaching can influence public policy. For him, it is not so much a question of whether or not there are principles that are perennial, but the role of principles—such as they are—in the political process. He sees the principles of Catholic social teaching as an important point of engagement with the world, not so much because they function as a means of resolving policy problems that cannot otherwise be adequately solved, but because they are effective in opening dialogue about problems in need of public policy solutions.

At the end we return to the witchetty grubs, with an epilogue by Frank Brennan, in which he draws on the remarks made by the other contributors and situates the discussion in the pressing challenge that constitutional recognition of Indigenous peoples poses, and the resources that Catholic social teaching might provide for rising to that challenge.

Catholic teaching and Australian politics

Australian political problems and Catholic policy solutions

Greg Craven

It comes as no surprise to hear that Australian politics is not short of problems at the moment. What is more surprising is to hear that Catholic policy solutions might be what the moment requires.

Often enough we hear about unfashionable Catholic moral teaching on marriage, abortion, sexuality, euthanasia, and the like—or 'special pleading' for Catholic schools—or the shameful behaviour of Catholic priests and the failure of church authorities that was exposed through the Royal Commission into Institutional Responses to Child Sexual Abuse. These all speak to serious challenges that contemporary politicians, churches, and Australian society at large need to address. What we hear less about, however, is the contribution that Catholic social teaching can make as a resource for addressing a whole range of policy problems that Australian governments need to tackle.

Australian political life is dominated by three broad approaches to public policymaking: liberalism, conservatism, and social democracy. Although the principles of Catholic social teaching resonate with aspects of each of these, they also offer a basis for providing a critique of all three approaches. More than that, however, the principles are themselves a resource that can help shape public policy in Australia. Some commentators will waste no time in decrying this suggestion as outrageous chutzpah. Surely, they will say, this is nothing but an extremely thinly veiled attempt to make Australian society 'more Catholic'.

Whether a 'more Catholic' Australia would be a good thing or a bad thing has very little to do, however, with the suggestion that Catholic social teaching could be a valuable resource for public policymaking in Australia. When its principles are properly understood, it becomes apparent why a Jewish Labour politician from Britain, such as Maurice Glasman, can describe it as a gift to the nations of the world. If nothing else, Catholic social teaching is a remarkably humane response to the challenges that attended the birth of modernity. These are challenges that we are still dealing with, and so any fair-minded person at least ought to be open to the possibility that it might have something valuable to offer.

I believe that a proper understanding of the principles of Catholic social teaching reveals that they are a resource of enduring utility, and one that can be put to good use in trying to address many of the policy problems that Australian politics currently struggles to resolve.

Catholic social teaching emerged in response to the economic, social, and political upheaval of the eighteenth and nineteenth centuries. During this time, centuries-old social structures were replaced by new and competing visions for organizing society and formulating what has since come to be called public policy. Arising from a combination of Enlightenment thought, the experience of revolution, and the impact of industrialisation, they formed the political traditions that remain prominent in Australian politics in the twenty-first century.

Following the industrialisation of Western economies in the nineteenth century, the significance of the social question was becoming apparent. In practice, liberal economic policy prompted disparities in wealth and influence between the owners of capital and labour. Workers were often paid dismally low wages and suffered through destitute living conditions. The tensions between capital's owners and the growing labour movement led to intense, sometimes even violent, labour unrest. With the experience of the French Revolution a not-too-distant memory, the ruling and capital-owning classes were particularly afraid of socialist threats to themselves and to the stability of society. As a result, there was a growing awareness of the social implications of economic policy in the nineteenth century. This awareness led people to look for answers to the social questions of their time, particularly as it concerned the treatment of workers. It was in this social and economic context that the intellectual and political battles between liberals, socialists, and conservatives were played out.[1]

In response to the ideological solutions to the political problems presented by these changing social and economic conditions, Pope Leo XIII's 1891 encyclical, *Rerum novarum*, marked a new undertaking for the Catholic Church. Previously, the church had refused to endorse or even engage with modern political ideologies. This was due, in part, to the political dependence of the church on established social structures and institutions, as well as the church's reaction to the massive and bloody assault made on it during the French Revolution.[2] Nevertheless, by the late nineteenth century Leo grew concerned that Catholic workers were increasingly abandoning the church to join socialist labour movements. More important, however, was the church's growing awareness of its responsibility to contribute an alternate vision for justice and cooperation in the organisation of modern society. Condemning the twin evils of unbridled capitalism and socialism was not going to be enough. The church needed to have an authoritative position on how a contemporary society could uphold justice for all. In *Rerum novarum* ('Of New Things'), Leo sought to address how Catholics should respond to the new social and political context. The encyclical's title reflects not only the subject of the encyclical—the new social and political changes—but also Leo's new approach of engagement rather than outright condemnation. As a result, *Rerum novarum* offers a new vision for a modern society that upholds longstanding Catholic principles about what makes a good society.

In *Rerum novarum*, Leo identifies and condemns the moral failures of the liberal policies that generate unjust societies, such as the commodifying of labour and undignified working conditions. Leo rejects the premise that there should be no political regulation of economic relations and instead affirms the moral duties of those who possess wealth to address the needs of the poor and working classes. He maintains that wages ought to be determined not by what we now call market signals, but instead by what is necessary to support labourers and their families beyond mere subsistence. His encyclical also strongly condemns collectivism, the abolition of private property, and class conflict as inadequate solutions to social injustice. Leo affirms the right to private property and gives conditional approval to market economics, provided it remains under the rule of law and at the service of the common good. He affirms the role of the state to interfere in economic spheres to defend the rights of the workers, including the right to be organized. He also uses *Rerum novarum* to affirm such principles as the rights of the weak and the dignity of work. He encourages the importance of professional associations, including labour organizations, and acknowledges the role of the state in the pursuit of the common good. Finally, he affirms free collaboration and cooperation in society as the solutions to social questions instead of class war.

At the heart of this encyclical is the conviction that unjust social conditions and social unrest are not just economic and political issues, but that they are caused by a failure to uphold moral and indeed ethical principles. Involved in this recognition is the conviction that a just society must be ordered towards the dignity of the human person and that it must allow each person to participate in the common good. It insists that human beings are both individuals, with rights proper to them that cannot be absorbed by a collective or for mutual benefit, and part of a community, with a duty to uphold the good of others. If the liberals insisted that economics ought to have the final say in the organization of the society, the socialists proclaimed the sovereignty of the collective state, and the reactionary conservatives claimed that nothing needed to change at all, *Rerum novarum* declared that the social question could only be answered by the free cooperation of all parties in society to act in the common good.

Since *Rerum novarum*, popes and church leaders have sought to apply Catholic moral teaching to changing social circumstances through a series of papal encyclicals and conciliar documents.[3] However, these ideas and principles have also found a wider audience. In the early twentieth century, they were systematised by English Catholic writers, Hilaire Belloc and G. K. Chesterton, into the economic theory of distributism.[4] Distributism sought to find a third way between capitalism and socialism. In the years following Chesterton and Belloc, however, it failed to catch on as a competitive alternative. Nevertheless, it continued to attract interest in Australia throughout the twentieth century, shaping strands of thinking in the Labor Party and drawing the attention of people interested in the application of Catholic social teaching, including influential political figures such as B. A. Santamaria and the political party he helped found, the Democratic Labour Party. Race Matthews, who was the chief of staff to Gough Whitlam, has remained a staunch proponent of distributism and has written about the important legacy it has in Victoria.[5] Outside Australia, distributism has also seen significant application in the Mondragón cooperative based in Spain, whose workers have shared ownership of their workplaces.

Through its systematisation in distributism, a larger audience was exposed to the principles espoused in *Rerum novarum*. Leo's precepts, such as the necessity of fair wages and the pursuit of the common good, became foundational in the thought of the labour movements of the early twentieth century, including in Australia. As a result, Catholic social teaching came to have an impact on Australian industrial relations, most notably in the landmark *Harvester* case of 1907, in which Justice Henry Bournes Higgins, no Catholic but clearly influenced by *Rerum novarum*, adjudicated on what would constitute 'fair and reasonable' wages under the *Excise Tariff Act 1906*. His verdict of 42 shillings to cover the needs of a worker's family of five was based on a combination of basic mathematics and the statement from *Rerum novarum* that "a workman's wages be sufficient to enable him comfortably to support himself, his wife, and his children."[6] Higgins drew on this in his judgement that remuneration "must be enough to support the wage earner in reasonable and frugal comfort." Although the influence was not explicitly acknowledged, there is no doubt from Higgins's wording that that Leo directly influenced him. The case resulted in the introduction of a basic weekly wage for workers and was foundational for the pay structure and the protection of workers in Australia. In the *Harvester* case, we can see a concrete historical example of how Catholic social teaching on economic justice was used as a resource for Australian public policymaking.

Over the last century and a quarter, Catholic social teaching has demonstrated an ability to develop as political and social conditions change over time and as different concerns rise to prominence. The goal of papal commentary on the organization of society, and its potential application to public policymaking, has been to bring the unchanging principles of the Catholic moral and social tradition to bear on changing politics and social circumstances. Thus, Catholic social teaching can serve to give guidance on modern political, economic, and social life, addressing issues of justice and charity in these spheres. Its evolving body of teaching addresses the contemporary issues that affect the social life of the human person, condemning what infringes upon the common good while affirming the dignity, freedom, and interdependence of human beings in changing social circumstances.

These principles emerge out of Catholic theology but do not depend on some monolithic acceptance of Catholic moral teaching. Instead, they are built on natural law principles that can be deduced through reasoning about human needs and aspirations to recognise the universal dignity and common good of humanity. Catholic social teaching's appeal to people outside the church marks a significant point of change in Catholic theology and history. This change is reflected in Pope John XXIII's 1963 encyclical, *Pacem in terris*, which is the first time that an ecclesial document was addressed to "all men of good will."[7] In doing so, the church recognises that the principles of its social doctrine are not founded solely on Christian belief, but in rational discernment that belongs to all who would seek truth and justice.

It is important to note what is meant here by the application of Catholic social teaching to public policymaking. It is not the same thing as the enforcement of all aspects of Catholic teaching, such as its teachings on revelation and theology in Australian politics and society. It does not mean theocracy. Any purchase it may have depends instead on discussion and persuasion. As a result, a society that adopts the principles of Catholic social teaching that we discuss here can quite legitimately be one that makes room for people who do not observe Catholic teaching in other aspects of their lives.[8] At its best, it is an exercise in urbanity.

Given that it emerges from a framework of moral principles, Catholic social teaching is also more than just a critique of contemporary political ideas: it contains a vision for human flourishing in social and political spheres. In doing so, Catholic social teaching cautions against viewing the market or the state alone as the primary means of recognising value or establishing social order. Instead, in Catholic social teaching, human institutions and traditions are affirmed, protected, and set towards the service of human dignity and participation in society. At the same time, the positive role of both markets and the state, when civilised and curtailed, is recognised, not as a good in itself, but as being in service to a good society. All of this is captured by four fundamental principles: the dignity of the human person, the common good, subsidiarity, and solidarity.

At the core of Catholic social teaching is *the dignity of the human person*. Emerging from the conviction that each of us is a beloved person created in the image and likeness of God, it emphasises the inherent good of each individual human being. To recognise this intrinsic dignity of the human person includes recognising the person as a unity of reason, freedom, and love. Recognising that each person possesses free will, rationality, and a capacity for solidarity with others, compels a society to also recognise and promote each person's rights and duties.

As a result, Catholic social teaching declares that a human being can never be treated as capital or with merely instrumental value. In the words of the 1965 conciliar document, *Gaudium et spes*, "The subject and the goal of all social institutions is and must be the human person."[9] This involves recognising that human beings are not merely units of labour or social problems but are free and responsible people with rights and obligations. From this core principle, the other principles of Catholic social teaching follow.

Emphasising the dignity of the human being, and the grave evil involved in the degradation of a person, is a central pillar of Catholic moral teaching. The emphasis of this principle in *Rerum novarum* comes in response to the degrading conditions faced by workers in the nineteenth century. Catholic social teaching identifies the existence of inhumane working conditions, the treatment of people as mere tools for profit, and the removal of freedoms, as injustices that demean the dignity of human beings and lead to an unjust society. Instead, it affirms the intrinsic value of a person's work and contribution to society, recognising that each person should have access to the necessary material and spiritual goods that make up human life.

Also crucial to Catholic social teaching is the pursuit of *the common good*. The focus on the common good is a recognition that the human being is not only sacrosanct as an individual, but social and interdependent. As a result, both the state and individuals have duties towards all the members of the society. Given that the dignity of all human beings is equal, this means recognising the equal claim that all human beings have to the means of living a good and fully human life. The common good in Catholic social teaching does not mean the greatest good for the greatest number in the way that utilitarian theories understand collective happiness. Rather, in the words of *Gaudium et spes*, the common good is "the sum total of social conditions which allow people, either as groups or as individuals, to reach their fulfilment more fully and more easily."[10]

The principle of the common good protects against policies, states, and economies that pursue ends that benefit only select individuals or privileged groups. In response, Catholic social teaching recognises that civil society exists for the good of all people and that the needs of all persons must be addressed by the society of which they are members. These needs constitute more than addressing a person's basic subsistence, including also their ability to participate properly in social life and to flourish.

Instead of a society in which people elevate their interests in competition and collide with one another, the common good seeks cooperation and the elevation of the needs of others. It recognises that all members of a society are responsible for the flourishing of the whole. The common good is achieved when individuals, intermediate groups, and governmental authorities cooperate, according to their capacities, to pursue conditions that respect human dignity and enable the flourishing of all. The primary purpose of government is the pursuit of the common good. It is the duty of government to see that the common good is upheld and, then, to intervene when it is disregarded for other ends. The pursuit of the common good is not just the domain of governing authorities, however, but the responsibility of every person. Each of us must direct our energies beyond our personal or sectional interests to the needs of others around us. The common good is an idea of shared responsibility for each other.

The third key idea in Catholic social teaching is the principle of *subsidiarity*. Subsidiarity is the principle by which society is organized so that decisions can be made at the level of the most local capable authority. Beyond questions of policy and authority, subsidiarity pertains to relationships of different bodies within civil society. Catholic social teaching's emphasis on subsidiarity answers those political ideologies that regard the expansion of the state and the collectivisation of property as a means of combatting social injustice. As a result, subsidiarity denounces those ideologies that draw power and influence into the hands of a few at the expense of the legitimate freedoms of individuals, families, and subsidiary communities. The principle both curtails the reach of the state and affirms the value of non-governmental organizations and institutions that stand in between the individual and the state.

Subsidiarity is, therefore, the principle by which governance in society should be organized, and by which policies concerning the appropriate spheres of action and authority should be formulated. It recognises that larger and more powerful authorities and institutions should not attempt to accomplish what smaller and more local associations can achieve. Subsidiarity involves, as far as is practically possible, pushing the responsibility for decision-making down to its lowest and most local levels.

It should be noted, however, that although transferring power away from a centralised state is an essential component of subsidiarity, it is not all that is required to achieve it. Subsidiarity also requires promoting communities, institutions, and, at the most basic level, the flourishing of the family unit, to enable participation, identity, and a natural sense of solidarity for vulnerable individuals. It is a critical component of the principle of subsidiarity that society recognises the importance of the family and the requirement that it should not have its functions replaced by the state or other agencies. Local participation is particularly emphasised as the means by which people's needs can be best recognised and immediately addressed. Intermediate bodies between the individual and the state, such as churches, unions, and charities, allow individuals to shape their society. Critical to subsidiarity is, therefore, the acknowledgement of the principle of participation, which promotes people's capacity to involve themselves in the pursuit of the common good.

Finally, Catholic social teaching proclaims the virtue of *solidarity*. Solidarity is the recognition of social interdependence and the obligation to aid and support those in society who are in need. Following from its emphasis on the common good, Catholic social teaching maintains that a society ought to be committed to the good of all within it because people are naturally interdependent. The mutual dependence of humanity means that, in the words of John Paul II, solidarity is not "a feeling of vague compassion or shallow distress at the misfortunes of others. It is a firm and persevering determination to commit oneself to the common good."[11] It is, perhaps, solidarity which is the least natural of Catholic social virtues to the modern, individualistic Western mind.

Solidarity seeks to go beyond empathy for the disadvantaged and towards action that addresses the needs of the poor. It affirms the need for cooperation—rather than conflict or competition—between the different classes or sections of society. The principle of solidarity is also affirmed in Catholic social teaching's discussion of the universal destination of goods, which reflects the social aspect and use of wealth for the good of others. In this way, solidarity is a virtue that enables human beings to partake of and share in material and spiritual goods. It recognises that the common good requires that we are responsible for, and obligated to help, all members of our society.

Solidarity ought to be expressed by a society's commitment to the poor and disadvantaged. This means prioritising a 'preference for the poor' in how public policy is implemented. More than just providing financial relief, solidarity demands a commitment to remedying unjust social systems that compromise the dignity of the person and have a disparate impact on the poor. Thus, solidarity can be upheld through public policymaking that regulates markets, prevents exploitation of individuals, and is committed to assisting those who lack the means to assist themselves.

All of these principles stand together indivisibly. For example, it is important to appreciate the crucial relationship between the principles of subsidiarity and solidarity. Subsidiarity without solidarity may encourage self-isolation and privatism, whereas solidarity without subsidiarity tends towards domineering statist social assistance. In terms of formulating public policy, a key theme of Catholic social teaching is how excessive use of state authority violates the principle of subsidiarity and thus infringes upon the freedom and initiative of individuals. This must be considered when evaluating potential public policy initiatives. The principle of subsidiarity calls for the proper balance of authority, and thus a better balance of interests, in public discussion and policy formulation. Catholic social teaching also recognises that there are appropriate occasions and avenues for the state to make policy so that it can protect the needs of its people. The state has a duty towards promoting the common good in harmonising the goods of different groups and individuals with the requirements of justice.

Although these principles of Catholic social teaching are intended to provide a comprehensive vision of how a society should be organized, they are also a basis for providing a critique of the three dominant approaches to public policymaking in Australia: conservatism, liberalism, and social democracy. Liberalism, conservatism, and social democracy all have a rich heritage in Australian political history and have been explored in the marvellous books written recently by Tim Wilson, Damien Freeman, and Adrian Pabst respectively. Each of these three approaches, having developed and evolved from the political traditions that informed the writing of *Rerum novarum*, has points of comparison and contention with Catholic social teaching.

Rerum novarum is unashamedly a robust critique of the strain of liberalism most prevalent in the nineteenth century—the *laissez-faire* worldview. This worldview in its purest form seeks to advance the liberty of the human person as an individual, limit the involvement of the state, and promote the role of free-market competition in determining economic policy. Because of its emphasis on the individual as the focus of social organization, liberalism tends to be less equipped to uphold solidarity and affirm the interconnectedness of human beings. Catholic social teaching argues that there is more to the just organization of society than adequate economic management and freedom of choice.

This criticism stems from the fact that liberalism lacks a vision of what the common good is outside of the empowerment of individuals to make their own choices, provided that they do not interfere with anyone else's ability to do so. As Tim Wilson writes in *The New Social Contract*, his book on liberalism in Australia, one of the critical weaknesses of liberalism is that it does not have a fundamental set of values and principles to organize social cohesion. By emphasising the individual's empowerment to make decisions for his or her own good, liberalism does not naturally identify moral values outside of equal opportunity of access to prosperity. It is good that society pursues prosperity, but, as Catholic social teaching maintains, it is not the primary end of human social endeavour. Pure liberalism relies on individuals to organize in their common interest without adequately promoting the solidarity required to underpin the kind of relationships that make up a good society.

Nevertheless, liberalism also prizes the distribution of power away from the bureaucracy of state control and into the hands of individuals. As Wilson argues, individuals are in the best position to determine their interests, not centralised governing bodies. On this matter, there is a substantial similarity with Catholic social teaching's emphasis on the principle of subsidiarity. Both strongly reject the centralised state as the best means of redistributive justice because of its lack of proximity to the needs of individuals. Policies that reduce the distance between the parties concerned and the decision-makers are better able to respond to people's needs.

Wilson makes a case for a distinctive form of Australian liberalism in *The New Social Contract* that is distinct from the pure liberalism of the nineteenth century. He argues that twenty-first-century Australian liberalism is a descendant of the *laissez-faire* liberalism of the nineteenth century, which, he concedes, advocated for the liberty of the individual, the limited involvement of the state and the role of free-market competition in determining economic policy. He argues, however, that contemporary Australian liberalism prioritises the liberty of the individual not just as an end in itself, but also so that individuals can be free to make decisions and to take responsibility for their welfare. The result of the promotion of egalitarian democracy, broad ownership of private property, and equality of opportunity is, according to Wilson, that every person can engage fruitfully in society. Wilson envisages a form of contemporary Australian liberalism that is not opposed to values of social justice, but which is directed towards ensuring equality of opportunity and protecting individuals from the external pressures that would compromise their ability to pursue the good life. Because he understands the individual to have a range of interests that need protection in order for the person to flourish, rather than merely having an interest in personal freedom, Wilson ends up providing a liberal defence of marriage, family life, and other social institutions. Only by promoting such a range of goods, he argues, can public policymaking be directed towards the empowerment of the individual.

Wilson argues against any "arbitrary obstacles" that

compromise an individual's ability to choose his or her best life.[12] His emphasis on the good of individuals, endowed with the dignity and responsibility to make choices in the interests of their own flourishing, is reminiscent of Catholic social teaching's emphasis on the centrality of the human person to the organization of society. Although he argues that liberalism, correctly understood, does not seek liberty as an end in itself, he acknowledges that, over the last fifty years, liberalism has prioritised advancing freedom, not just for the individual, but also for the sake of enterprise, capital, mobility, and technology. As a result, when liberalism's priority shifts away from the interests of the whole human person, it is susceptible to the danger of focusing too heavily on the freedom of open economic transaction and efficiency, often as a system in itself, in place of the people it is meant to serve. This is a danger that Wilson sharply criticises, but one that is inherent in the kind of liberalism that sees the prime duty of just society as encouraging enterprise and prosperity.

Wilson argues that one of the strengths of liberalism is that it does not seek to prioritise the interests of one section of society over any other. Although its vision of a society organized for the empowerment of the individual and equal opportunity does respect the dignity of the human person, this emphasis conflicts with *Rerum novarum's* insistence that "In protecting the rights of private individuals, however, special consideration must be given to the weak and the poor."[13] A just society requires support for those whose circumstances mean that they cannot achieve a good life by themselves. Moreover, a just society needs to meet more than people's material needs. People need a sense of place, allegiance to 'little platoons', and a sense of the dignity of their work and endeavours. Although Wilson distinguishes his presentation of liberalism from the pure liberalism of previous centuries, this liberalism is still relatively poorly equipped to shape policymaking that meets the demands of the common good and encourages solidarity.

The emergence of liberalism in the eighteenth and nineteenth centuries prompted denunciation from political conservatives seeking to hold onto the traditional organization of society. However, it was in Edmund Burke, the great eighteenth-century English politician and political theorist widely regarded by modern conservatives as their intellectual father, that conservatives find an antecedent who, though hostile to radicalism, was in no sense reactionary. In his *Reflections on the Revolution in France*, Burke emphasises the centrality of shared values that are ingrained within a society's political tradition, and which are lived out by its members in their communities and institutions. In *Abbott's Right*, Damien Freeman identifies the uniquely Australian strain of conservatism that can be traced back to Burke, as prioritising both "individual freedom and communal institutions." This approach to politics looks to respond to change with public policymaking that is guided by the values of Australian society and tradition, rather than being guided by abstract theorising.[14] The social liberal-conservatism of Australia's second prime minister, Alfred Deakin, was as much the child of Burke as were any Menzies or Fraser.

Conservatism's high regard for the role of institutions in shaping public life aligns with Catholic social teaching's emphasis on subsidiarity. Both conservatism and Catholic social teaching identify communities and institutions as the primary and most effective locus for social change and human flourishing. Freeman quotes former prime minister Tony Abbott when he explains that Australian conservatism places its emphasis not on individuals or the collective but on the "relationships between people and institutions which are the making of both."[15] As a result, Australian conservatism also shares much of Catholic social teaching's criticism of socialism and the dangers of the state's overreach. Freeman writes that substantial state intervention diminishes both the flourishing of the individual and the functioning of institutions and communities.

Conservatism also shares Catholic social teaching's critique of individualistic liberalism and instead seeks to identify and apply the values inherent within the society to public policymaking. Conservatism's respect for the values of a national tradition as a guiding principle for future public policymaking is consistent with Catholic social teaching's emphasis on the pursuit of a just society in which the dignity of the human person is prioritised. Australian conservatism, as articulated by Freeman, highlights shared values ingrained within the Australian tradition, such as the 'fair go', love of the country, and a uniquely Australian commitment to equality.

However, a noteworthy point of critique that Catholic social teaching has of conservatism is in their differing visions of the common good. The conservative vision of the common good is significantly weaker when compared to what is outlined in Catholic social teaching. Although Catholic social teaching would agree with Freeman's assessment that its pursuit ought to be the goal of all public policy, it has a richer definition of what the common good is and how it ought to be pursued. Freeman defines the common good as being anything that is "shared by or beneficial to all" members of the society.[16] Within the framework of conservatism, this signifies promoting those things within the national tradition that work for the good and prosperity of the people in a society, be it the free market or nationally held values. In Catholic social teaching, however, the common good is understood to consist of more than just socio-economic wellbeing or upholding common values to include harmonising different interests in accordance with those values that promote human dignity.

Freeman notes that conservatism, unlike pure liberalism, acknowledges that there are occasions when critical components of a nation's political tradition, such as free-market economic policies, ought to be discarded if they no longer serve the common good. However, conservatism's emphasis on the guiding role of tradition means that it can fail to recognise times and places when change is required. Although Freeman notes, following Burke, that conservatism is open to changes in public policy that preserve the society's values, it can remain unresponsive to the call for justice and solidarity from people currently disadvantaged by the way the society is organized. Freeman highlights some examples of this in Australian history, identifying Malcolm Fraser's upholding of the Australia Settlement in the early 1980s as an occasion when necessary adaptations to the changing economic situation were not made. At this point, conservative policymaking can descend into becoming mere resistance to change and can fall into defending unjust social systems and traditions.

Michael Quinlan, an Australian academic lawyer, also has reservations about Freeman's treatment of 'values'.[17] Freeman identifies the "values of the Australian tradition" as being important to Australian conservatism. However, Quinlan argues that it is not enough for a just society to have just any values and traditions, but that it ought to uphold Judeo-Christian values and traditions. Quinlan maintains that Freeman fails to identify any positive universal goods promoted by this approach to conservatism. This indicates that conservatives can fall into the trap of not reflecting critically on the content of their values, traditions, and institutions. As a result, conservativism can fall into being too vague as to what these values and traditions actually are and how they apply to contemporary policymaking or, alternatively, overlook the fact that these values and traditions may be causing injustices in the society. This would contravene Catholic social teaching's emphasis on the importance of the particular principles, such as solidarity and subsidiarity, that ought to be promoted in a just society irrespective of its tradition or institutions.

Whereas liberalism emerged in the eighteenth century as an alternative for social reform that catered predominantly to the emerging middle class, and was resisted by conservatives in ruling classes looking to maintain traditional values and structures, social democracy emerged as an alternative agenda for reform that catered predominantly to the working class. Social democracy draws on the tradition of the nineteenth-century labour movement in pushing for public policymaking that advocated for the rights and interests of the workers and the poor, perhaps more than it draws on the socialism of the nineteenth century that appealed to the same labour base.

Adrian Pabst argues in *Story of Our Country* that, contrary to the socialism of Karl Marx, Australian social democracy promotes a regulated market economy that can work within frameworks of economic justice, social cohesion, and the national interest.

Pabst argues that social democracy seeks to defend the interests of working people through public policymaking that emphasises enabling people from all circumstances to pursue the common good and to have a share in the good life. One of the goals of social democracy is, in Pabst's words, to "civilise capitalism" by making sure that prosperity and free enterprise never comes at the expense of other human beings.[18] As a result, social democracy aims to ensure what Paul Keating called the "social graft of the market economy" that upholds economic fairness and people's security.[19]

Pabst's conception of contemporary Australian social democracy treats the common good, as explicitly inspired by *Rerum novarum* and Catholic social teaching, as the core value of public policymaking. A critical component of social democracy's approach to the common good is its commitment to the fair treatment and remuneration of labour. In this regard, there is a considerable resemblance to Catholic social teaching's principle of solidarity and the preferential option for the poor, especially with the poorest and neediest of society.

However, social democracy is vulnerable to conceiving of political solutions only through governmental and party participation means, seeing its advocacy of the needs of the poor as a relationship between individuals and representatives of the state. By doing so, it runs the risk of compromising the principle of subsidiarity. Although social democracy has always upheld the importance of the labour movement's ability to form independent institutions and unions, it still relies too heavily on lobbying for governmental enforcement of justice instead of empowering local institutions and private initiatives.

In response, Catholic social teaching would emphasise attempting to foster initiative and empowerment at lower levels of authority (which is precisely the experience from which today's labour movement grew). Solidarity without subsidiarity can suppress effective participation in civil society and, thus, the individual's pursuit of the common good. Select interests should not receive preferential treatment, nor should governments seek to foster dependence on state resources. Governmental overreach, according to Pope John Paul II, relegates the human person to becoming an "object of state administration" that absorbs the personal and local initiative necessary to a sense of human dignity.[20]

In overemphasising the need for social change through centralised public policymaking, contemporary Australian social democracy risks destabilising the economic and social security that ordinary people in society seek. This is a feature of modern left-wing politics that Pabst strongly argues against, claiming that one of the strengths of social democracy in Australia is its ability to recognise the socially ('small-c') conservative values of its base. These people depend on the stability and security of traditional family and community institutions for their prosperity. When combined with the tendency towards centralised managerialism, contemporary social democracy risks becoming disconnected from the immediate needs of the poor. The tension between 'climate action' and the preservation of jobs is an obvious instance of this tendency.

Frank Bongiorno, an historian of the labour movement in Australia, observes that Pabst's book highlights how social democracy in Australia, especially within the Labor Party, has abandoned its traditional working-class constituency.[21] Bongiorno argues that this has happened because economic and social change has meant that the families and communities that formed around a unionised labour-intensive workforce do not exist as they used to. Bongiorno also quotes the ALP's review of its 2019 election loss, which highlighted how focussing on the needs of one constituency is a significant problem for Australian social democracy: "The dilemma is not easy to resolve. It cannot be resolved simply by choosing one constituency over another." As a result, Bongiorno argues that Pabst's proposal for social democracy does not fix the problem either, primarily because it advocates for the needs of an expiring constituency and so does not adequately address the needs or values of contemporary Australians.

Bongiorno's criticisms highlight how Pabst's formulation of social democracy is also guilty of neglecting what Catholic social teaching would identify as the common good and the requirements of solidarity. Given the social and economic change in Australian society, Pabst's idea of social democracy may no longer adequately address the needs of the poor, and would therefore no longer uphold the principle of solidarity. A politics that does not address the needs of a constituency as it exists is bad politics. Just like the policy measures of the more progressive elements of social democracy, Pabst's vision may overlook the concrete needs and circumstances of the poor in service to a political ideology. Here, social democracy may conflict with Catholic social teaching's emphasis on public policymaking that serves the common good in that, while it preferences the needs of the poor, it also needs to appeal beyond sectional interests to the good of the whole society.

The different emphases of each of Australia's most prominent political traditions, when evaluated using the principles of Catholic social teaching, inevitably contribute their strengths and weaknesses to the political landscape as it exists today. It may be somewhat surprising to note that, at a more fundamental level, all three of these approaches to public policymaking are currently suffering from a common problem. In the last thirty years, it has become increasingly challenging to determine what principles motivate policy in Australian politics. The existing disconnect between principles and policy makes it hard to deduce whether any cohesive framework of principles still underpins twenty-first-century Australian public policymaking. Whatever good might come from contrasting our most influential political traditions, there is little point if we cannot identify the fundamental principles that shape their approaches to policymaking.

Simply put, sound principles direct public policy towards people's wellbeing. By grounding itself in an anthropological understanding of what it means to be a human being in a community of other human beings, such a framework enables us to generate policies that advance the common good and uphold the requirements of justice. This is because a good framework of principles helps to identify the kind of society in which we would actually want to live. It does this by recognising what essential human needs and values lie behind any given political issue. A framework of principles, thus helps policymakers pinpoint what human benefit their policy is intended to serve and, then, shape their policy to achieve this.

For example, when formulating policies for education, all are agreed that it would be good to have a high quality of education for all, even for those who would be unlikely to reap the full benefits of it. But how do we answer why this is a good thing and why people benefit from universal quality education? Not being able to answer this question has an impact on our ability to recognise what concrete good this policy is trying to achieve. We shall return to this question later, but this kind of question lies underneath all political decision-making.

A framework of principles is not just an assortment of disconnected values or the elevation of one good to the neglect of others. Freeman is correct to argue in *Abbott's Right* that ideologies enslave the multiplicity of values under one virtue, whether that be liberty, security, or equality. As a result, we ought to ask what criteria policymakers can draw on to discern between different values when it comes to policymaking. What is required is a cohesive framework of principles that can address the complicated and seemingly contradictory assortment of needs and priorities present in any society.

However, lacking a cohesive framework of principles presents real challenges for answering these questions, especially when all of the policy options available exact a heavy price. In the absence of a vision for the kind of society that we would want to live in, policymaking in this environment tends to become transactional. Although Wilson, Freeman, and Pabst each attempt to outline a principled basis for their approaches to policymaking, Australian politics in the last thirty years has been more likely to be informed by a kind of disconnected pragmatism than by a framework of principles. At its best, transactional politics is at least responsive to a general impression of what we want a given policy to achieve. However, at its worst, this kind of transactionalism often amounts to little more than a trade-off between a politician and special interest groups; one that exchanges votes and political support for a different shuffling of resources. This is the politics of short-term targets and wins that is in danger of turning politics in this country into a mere process of picking political winners and losers.

Instead of policy decisions that are anchored in a set of principles that give it long-term direction, the policymaking process in Australia today is hypersensitive to whatever can improve the political transaction, in both the short and long terms. For this reason, some important policies in recent years have been the products either of spontaneous or incremental decision-making. In recent decades, numerous policies have been drawn up in immediate reaction to some crisis or loss in an opinion poll with the hope of regaining short-term popularity. At the other extreme, several policies have suffered repeated tinkering, prompted by the need to pick different winners and losers, to the extent that the original purpose of the policy has been lost. There are significant dangers in both tendencies that stem from not articulating a cohesive framework of principles, as has been repeatedly borne out in the way that critical problems have been approached.

Normal democratic compromise and grubby politics are one thing, but policies that are designed with the goal of gaining the support of key interest groups or to achieve impressive sounding targets are not likely to be policies that benefit the whole society. Without principles that identify what common human needs are the purpose of a policy, policymaking will be distracted by interests and goals that, even if they are well intentioned, do no concrete good.

Since 1990, in addition to the prevalence of transactional pragmatism in our public policy, Australian society has seen a pronounced weakening in shared values and mutual obligation. The sense in which citizens recognise their part in contributing to the good of every other Australian is dissolving into identity politics and isolation. The decline in agreed moral obligations and principles, outside of special pleading for individual or tribal gain, is not just a political problem in Australia, but a social one as well. The weakening of a sense of mutual obligation has prevented Australian political discourse from identifying a framework of principles that we all hold in common that can be directed towards an agreed common good. The rise of identity politics also has produced myriad micro-constituencies each focussed on highly particular issues to the exclusion of any synthetic understanding of a wider common good.

These are fundamental problems in the way we go about politics in contemporary Australia and are not just problems with one particular political tradition. By contrast, there is a framework of principles within Catholic social teaching that would provide an antidote to pragmatic and transactional approaches to politics. In the words of Pope Benedict XVI, the principles of Catholic social teaching can, as more than just a tool for critiquing existing politics, be a resource that helps to "purify reason and to contribute, here and now, to the acknowledgement and attainment of what is just."[22] This vision can motivate a better way to go about politics in Australia. Concentrating policymaking on fundamental propositions about the nature of human beings and the mutual obligations that we have towards one another enables Catholic social teaching to arrive at principles that can then shape sound public policymaking.

Policymaking informed by Catholic social teaching begins by recognising the dignity of the human person. This principle directs all policymaking to what upholds or neglects the intrinsic value of human beings. Having this principle as the centrepiece of a framework of principles helps us to determine how all the seemingly contradictory interests of public policy, such as efficiency, security, equality, and liberty, might be reconciled and directed towards the good of individuals and the common good. Because of the influence of this understanding of human dignity in Catholic social teaching's framework of principles, we can see how the other principles of Catholic social teaching differ from seemingly similar political values. For example, we can draw a clear contrast between the Catholic and the utilitarian understandings of the common good. While the utilitarian principle aims to achieve the greatest good for the greatest number, the Catholic understanding of the common good looks to the duties that the nation has towards meeting the needs of the whole society. This distinction directs policymaking from cost-benefit analyses towards identifying what needs everyone in our society has in common.

In another example of how the principles of Catholic social teaching are different, the principle of subsidiarity is not a kind of Catholic libertarianism. Instead, it underpins the natural good of different levels of authority for different ends, allowing policymakers to consider what level of decision-making is most effective. Likewise, the principle of solidarity is not just a demand for fairness or equality, but a principle that informs how policy ought to be directed towards our mutual obligations to each other, especially those most in need. All of these values help direct our thinking about politics towards a vision of a just society of the kind in which we would want to participate.

As we have seen, part of the difficulty in assembling a framework of principles for formulating public policy lies in addressing the apparent conflicts of values. At first glance, applying the principles of Catholic social teaching would appear to hold the same difficulties. How can policymakers reconcile the principle of subsidiarity with the state's role in ensuring the common good? How can the emphasis on the good of the individual human being be applied at the same time as the principle of solidarity which calls for the recognition of the good of the community? Part of the genius of Catholic social teaching, however, is its ability to hold its principles in creative tension, a capacity notably under-rated in Australian political discourse, with its obsession with 'winning' and 'losing', despite the fact that it is intrinsic to such Australian constitutional staples as responsible government and federalism. For example,

Catholic social teaching approaches the tricky balance between localising decision-making and the need for national schemes for healthcare or education by emphasising both subsidiarity and solidarity. These two principles, when left in creative tension, can move a society towards the inherent good in attempting to localise decision-making while also recognising the inherent good of the resources of the nation being employed for common benefit.

In addition, whereas Australian society has witnessed a weakening of a sense of mutual obligation, an essential element of Catholic social teaching since *Rerum novarum* has been to recall the mutual obligations that we share because of our common human nature. Catholic social teaching helps us make political decisions that are based on shared human needs rather than identity politics or support for interest groups. What identity is claimed or whose tribe is favoured ought not to be the decisive factor in formulating policies for the common good.

What we see here is how the framework of principles in Catholic social teaching helps us to get to the bottom of what good a policy is supposed to achieve by answering the critical 'why' questions that support political decision-making. As a result, Catholic social teaching has the potential to provide a strong mesh that would undergird policymaking in Australia. By applying the principles of human dignity, the common good, subsidiarity, and solidarity to public policymaking, we can develop a sense of what matters most for the pursuit of the flourishing of the Australian people. Its cohesive framework of principles helps us first to address what the real good of the society is, and then identify how it can best be pursued. The challenge of improving Australia's education system provides an excellent example of how the principles of Catholic social teaching can be a resource for Australian politics. The problems besetting education policymaking in Australia today include such issues as falling results, schools being under-resourced, the ineffective use of available resources, and the disparity in the quality of schools. At the policy level, this involves making decisions about how curricula are developed, what resources are selected, where funding is prioritised, and to whom it is directed.

In response to these problems, politicians have proposed several possible solutions. One has been a general increase in school funding across the board, such as under Kevin Rudd's National Plan for School Improvement. Scores of critics, including Jennifer Hewett from the *Australian Financial Review*, Peter Goss from the Grattan Institute and former Education Minister Simon Birmingham, have criticised this solution by noting there has been "no simple relationship between overall spending on education and the level of student performance." They argue that general increases in education spending exacerbate the disparities between poorer and richer schools. Other proposed solutions, such as the Rudd government's Digital Education Revolution, or Malcolm Turnbull's National Innovation and Science Agenda, have attempted to target funding to specific educational areas, such as to information technology skills or scientific, technological, engineering, and mathematical fields. Commentators suggest these solutions have not sufficiently addressed the challenges either: as Glenn Fahey wrote in the *Australian Financial*

Review of Rudd's Digital Education Revolution, "while we have more computers, there's no evidence they're transforming education." Another potential solution has been to introduce a broader curriculum with more subjects and learning outcomes. However, as a senior research fellow at Australian Catholic University, Kevin Donnelly, noted, the result of this initiative has been an overcrowded and shallow curriculum that fails to focus on essential learning and educational standards.

Acknowledging the good intentions that went into these policies, these criticisms highlight the fact that these policies may not have been designed by identifying the purpose of education but instead by identifying what resources could be added and where they could be added to. Transactional politics fails to identify what human good will be advanced and instead focuses on resource allocation. This has happened because the fundamental questions underlying debates on educational reform have remained unasked and unanswered. The first question that a policymaker needs to ask about education ought to be: Why are we trying to provide a universal system of quality education? There is a series of other fundamental questions that follow from this one. For example, what do we want students to gain from their schooling? Why provide quality education for difficult cases who are not going to benefit from it? Answering these questions provides the launchpad for thinking beyond the transactional cost-benefit analysis attempts at policymaking that have become habitual in Australian politics. Questions of this kind can only be answered by applying a cohesive framework of principles to the challenge of education.

If the crucial question, "Why universal quality education?"

were to be addressed using the framework of Catholic social teaching's principles, we might begin by applying the principle of human dignity. This principle prompts us to say that individual human beings are immensely valuable, no matter what other attributes they do or do not have, and that for this reason alone, their formation is good in and of itself—not as a means to any particular end. The primary goal of our education system, then, is the formation of individual human beings. From this foundation, we can start to address the problem of the disparity in educational standards across the country. By recognising that the good of education lies primarily in the intrinsic good of forming individual human beings and providing them with capacities to improve their own lives, rather than regarding an investment in young people as something for which the nation expects to receive a return, we can deduce that we need to supply a good standard of education to every student.

This kind of thinking also avoids a 'general spending' approach or a broad implantation of standards because it demands that we think about what things are essential to human formation, which are not going to be the same for every student or every school. This would require schools to have the freedom to be able to respond to their immediate needs, and not just to nationally determined criteria. This is where educational policy also needs to be informed by the principle of subsidiarity. There has been a lamentable waste of time and money spent on government mandates for schools that the people on the ground know to be unnecessary or unhelpful. This top-down, administration-overload approach has stifled schools into meeting unnecessary criteria and has drawn teachers' attention away from teaching and onto paperwork. The principle of subsidiarity would help us avoid a monolithic system of education that does not allow for variation or responsiveness to the needs of students and teachers.

This community-based approach allows the educational system to engage in solidarity. It promotes the lowest natural locus for decision-making that subsequently bases educational decision-making in communities with local solidarity. Rather than a bureaucracy that attempts to impose a pattern according to which all schools should function, decision-making can be more centred on the relationships and resources that arise from within the school community. As a result, schools can become places that grow from and support communities, with participation from people outside the immediate educational system.

One example of how a principled approach, based on Catholic social teaching, would shape better education policy involves the issue of teacher quality, an issue that I dealt with in my role as Chairman of the Teacher Education Ministerial Advisory Group, which reported in 2015. Maintaining the quality of teachers is obviously critical to a good education system, but most of the proposed methods of achieving this are incredibly problematic. Calls to enforce teacher standards at university entry by escalating minimum ATARs fail to recognise the extent to which a prospective teacher's ATAR is impacted by socioeconomic status. ATARs have very little to do with the competency of teachers when they graduate years later. The group proposed, in our 2015 report, that teacher quality could be better ensured through comprehensive performance testing and better practical experience during a teacher's education and training. The problem is not a low-quality intake, but poor enforcement of standards in the outtake. A test that everyone passes is a flawed test. A better education process allows people from tougher environments and lower socioeconomic status to have a chance to develop into better teachers. What we can see in this proposal is how recognising the dignity of trainee teachers, by ensuring quality training and removing barriers to success, leads us to better realise the common good of quality education. This also shows greater solidarity with people from lower SES backgrounds while also avoiding the kind of top-down regulation of entry that is discouraged by the principle of subsidiarity.

I acknowledge that our discussion is just a starting point for how Catholic social teaching would be a resource for formulating educational policy but starting with these principles will correct many of the problems that transactional politics has caused for the education system. A framework of principles that acknowledges what helps human beings to prosper and identifies the underlying purpose of the task at hand leads to policies that are directed towards a society where people have a greater chance to flourish. In this case, it means identifying education as the formation of young people and that, as a result, policies should be formulated to prioritise this good. Other challenges in contemporary Australian politics can be approached in a similarly principled way. Just as with education policy, if we can get behind the current political melees to identify the critical questions at the heart of each challenge, we can then apply the principles of Catholic social teaching to help identify the core issues. Such challenges abound in healthcare, aged care, and indigenous affairs.

The fundamental problem for healthcare and aged care policy in an aging population is to determine how to provide quality healthcare and how to allocate limited resources. One proposed solution has been for the federal government to take charge with a broad injection of funding for healthcare and aged care, as the Morrison government did in 2018 with the Community Health and Hospitals Program. The Grattan Institute's Stephen Duckett criticised this approach as "electoral expediency"[23] that was uncertain of what the policy was funding, what it was supposed to achieve, and whether it conflicted with the jurisdiction of the States. An alternative solution taken in recent decades has been to privatise healthcare and aged care and so cut taxpayer spending on healthcare. However, Lesley Russell of the University of Sydney criticised this approach in a piece for *The Conversation*, in which she highlighted how the lack of governmental involvement in healthcare would mean inadequate enforcement of health standards as well as blowing out private healthcare costs.

Both approaches, once again, dissolve the policy issues into economic trade-offs and confusion about the appropriate levels of authority. Underlying the issue of healthcare and aged care, however, is the question, 'Why do we try to provide high quality and expensive healthcare even for people who are close to death or who will not recover?' This question, which is at the core of the issue, can be approached and answered through the principles of Catholic social teaching. Again, we begin with the inviolable dignity of the human person as the starting point for healthcare in a just society. Recognising the dignity of the human being prompts recognition that we provide healthcare, not just because it benefits society to have healthy people, but because of the intrinsic good of human life. Recently, this issue has been presented starkly in the context of the value to be placed on the lives of the very elderly in the context of Covid-19. Can one discount the last few month of the life of a nonagenarian against the future longevity of a teenager, simply because one has longer to live than another? Or does the irreducible value of the human being protect both equally? In many senses, this question underlies much of future health economics.

By placing emphasis on the dignity of the individual human being at the outset, healthcare policies ought to be primarily attentive to the healthcare needs of the individual patient. Healthcare policy should also be attentive to the requirements of the common good, rather than being determined, as it often is, by 'greatest good for the greatest number' approaches. Healthcare and aged care policies should be responsive to the needs of those most dependent on healthcare to live. Just as *Rerum novarum* called for more than subsistence wages, healthcare and aged care should aim to help the sick and elderly lead something more than just subsistent lives. Crucially, there also needs to be recognition of our solidarity with the sick and aging. They are not 'other' or a 'burden' on the society but fellow human beings, deserving of continued support and care.

One example of how the principles of Catholic social teaching could be beneficial to healthcare policymaking would be in response to the crisis that has been caused by the lack of adequate and consistent staffing in aged care homes, as detailed in 2020 as part of the Royal Commission into Aged Care Quality and Safety's interim report. The royal commission has heard that aged care workers often experience excessive work demands that result in high staff turnover and a casual workforce within aged care. Not only does the casualisation of the aged care workforce diminish the quality of care, but it also exacerbated the Covid-19 crisis in aged care homes where it became standard practice for workers to work across multiple sites.

Although the royal commission can identify the correspondence between overworked, under-trained, transient, and casual staff and poor-quality care, a principled approach would never have allowed things to be set up in this way. Recognition of the dignity of both those in care and the staff that care for them involves acknowledging that understaffing and a casual workforce both diminishes the necessary human connection and familiarity with relationship-based care and creates dangerous working conditions. Under these conditions, authentic solidarity, and the interpersonal connection that it encourages, is impossible. The alternative, guided by the principles of Catholic social teaching, would involve prioritising the human element of aged care through models that would encourage more extensive training and less movement between facilities for aged care workers. The principles of Catholic social teaching reflect what one submission to the royal commission highlighted as the need to be "connecting with residents in order to see to their needs and to interact with them as people."[24]

Another critical issue in contemporary Australian politics

involves how best to achieve recognition and protection of Indigenous peoples. One solution put forward is to enact a treaty between Indigenous people and the Australian government. That would, in theory, recognise the sovereignty of Indigenous peoples and would establish agreed protections and rights. However, the treaty proposal has been criticised from a range of perspectives that include concerns, expressed by former prime ministers John Howard and Tony Abbott, that it would divide Australia into two nations and, as expressed by CEO of the Kimberley Land Council, Nolan Hunter, the damage that would be caused to other potential reforms by this unrealistic proposal. Nevertheless, Howard's alternative proposal of including recognition of Indigenous peoples in a preamble to the Australian Constitution has also been criticised by Indigenous leaders as being merely a symbolic gesture that would undermine meaningful change as well as potentially undermining the Constitution as a practical working document.

However, the principles of Catholic social teaching could again get behind the issue at hand to ask and answer the crucial 'why' question, which in this case involves answering why Indigenous peoples want recognition and meaningful change. The starting point for all discussions of Indigenous rights and recognition is the basic fact that these people are indeed people, entitled to a dignity that has often remained unrecognised. As a result, at the forefront of all Indigenous recognition is the imperative to ensure that the dignity of Indigenous people is consistently upheld. An insistence upon the common good tells us that this is an imperative not only for our Indigenous brothers and sisters but also ourselves and our own. Our 'Common-wealth' (or weal) is substantively diminished by a wilful ignoring of a vital part of our community and, as a result, we are less the nation we could be. This is also affirmed by the principle of solidarity, which dissolves the terrible non-distinction between 'them and us' and pursues the hope of an Australia where all members see themselves and their rights as being represented.

An alternative to the proposals stated above that would better lend itself to the application of Catholic social teaching is the creation of an 'Indigenous Voice' in the Australian Constitution. A 'voiceless person' is a contradiction in terms and represents a failure to recognise the dignity of that person. However, the exclusion of a substantive observance of Indigenous people from the mouth of our Constitution produces precisely this result. Constitutionally, the "whispering in our hearts" is silenced. As a result, far from surrendering part of our sovereignty, having meaningful recognition of the voices of Indigenous people means that we would be properly pursuing the common good that would allow our nation to grasp a yet greater potential. The principle of solidarity helps us to recognise that constitutional recognition is not a battle between enemies but a great continuation of the constitutional union offered in 1900 that sought to bring the people of this continent together as a united people. Australia is not compelled to further recognition of Indigenous people but pursues that cause because it is right and just and recognises the duties that we have to each other that arise from our mutual obligations. Finally, could there be a more rational instance of subsidiarity than authorising the voice and responsibility of those naturally best equipped and informed to make decisions, through the Indigenous voice, to speak, but not to dictate, upon matters of importance to Indigenous people? The principles of Catholic social teaching anchor a recognition of an Indigenous voice in Australia's Constitution.

These policy solutions demonstrate just how Catholic social teaching can shape public policymaking for contemporary Australian political issues. They also demonstrate that Catholic social teaching is not about supporting policy agendas that would benefit only the Catholic Church, but that it is about a framework of principles, developed from a sense of our common nature as human beings, that would enable a more just society.

Nevertheless, some might remain unconvinced that Catholic social teaching could really be the solution to much of what ails policymaking in twenty-first-century Australia. 'Catholic social teaching is all well and good,' they might say, 'but what unique goods does it achieve that can't be promoted by another political philosophy?' Indeed, there are not too many people who would deny that upholding the dignity of the human person is a good thing for a society, or that politics ought to pursue justice and the common good. We can all, at the very least, agree on the general 'vibe' of what we would like to see in our society. We would all like to see more justice, more equality, more liberty, more efficiency in Australian society. However, the fact that applying our common political vibe breaks down the second we introduce concrete political problems suggests that problems remain with how we approach politics.

Take any of the three prominent political traditions discussed in this essay. All three of them have emphases that have clear benefits for society and that, if pursued, would lead policymaking in a good direction. Even transactional politics can identify solutions that a great majority of us would agree ought to be 'winners'. The trade-offs between policymakers and interest groups can lead to some net wins for society. And yet, these approaches will always promote one principle to the exclusion of others. This is what devalues a robust concept like the common good into 'the greatest good for the greatest number', or subsidiarity into anti-government interference. What this means is that policymaking will tend towards solutions that either advance one value to the exclusion of all others, like an ideology, or try to meld together a policy that appeases any number of competing ideologies, like transactional politics.

For these reasons, the cohesive framework of principles behind Catholic social teaching serves as a unique kind of approach to public policymaking. Not only has Catholic social teaching strongly defined and developed principles, but it holds them in a creative tension that does not diminish their potency. Working within the framework of this tradition means that, instead of picking winners and losers or selecting what principles would work the best for a given issue, we can find a solution that meets all of the requirements of a just society. Catholic social teaching avoids the problems of transactional politics, as well as the failings of our traditional approaches to politics in Australia. It allows policymaking to be shaped by well thought out principles that allow us to build a deeper understanding of what needs lie behind Australia's most pressing political issues.

Responding to Greg Craven

1.

Teaching for best selves not best governments

Tony Abbott

LIKE GREG CRAVEN, the distinguished former vice-chancellor of Australian Catholic University, I take Catholicism seriously and hope to be 'my best self' in ways that are pleasing to God. I'm less convinced than Greg that the church has unique expertise in public life (as opposed to faith and morals) and doubt that Catholic social teaching can give definitive and compelling answers to contentious political issues. There's no doubt that the church has an immense contribution to make to building a better world, but I suspect that this lies much more in the 'formation' of the individuals who participate in public life than in providing specific 'Catholic answers' to the issues it throws up.

Although Catholic social teaching is supposed to be based on reason rather than revelation, and therefore to be accessible to "all men of goodwill", I doubt anyone reading an encyclical could mistake it for anything other than a church document. I agree with Craven that public policy should indeed respect the dignity of the human person, strive to realise the common good, be formulated and implemented as close to the people impacted as possible, and appreciate that the diminution of any person impacts on everyone (as Catholic social teaching holds). But although these fragrant principles should certainly rule *out* some policies, I'm not sure how far they can take us in ruling *in* any particular policy. Even if the church could devise uniquely persuasive approaches to public policy issues, I fear that explicitly basing them on Catholic social teaching might be counter-productive in a society where less than 25% identify as Catholic and weekly Mass attendance is about 10% at best.

Thanks to an education first with the Brigidine sisters at Holy Family School Lindfield (in the days when the teachers were all nuns), and then with the Jesuits at St Aloysius College Milson's Point and St Ignatius College Riverview (in the days when many of the teachers were still Jesuit priests and brothers), I reckon I gained a pretty good grounding in the essence of our faith.

Still reverberating forty years on, is the Gospel injunction "to love the Lord your God with your whole heart and your whole soul and your whole mind . . . and to love your neighbour as you love yourself . . . for on these two commandments hang all the law and the prophets" (Matthew 22:37-40). Put simply, my take from a Catholic education is that the best way to get close to God is frequent attendance at Mass and the other sacraments; and the best way to live a good life is always striving to treat others as you would have them treat you. Other than the famous advice to give governments their due, Jesus had nothing directly to say about public life.

Like a flashing neon light, of course, is the Gospel admonition to the rich young man who wanted to be perfect: to sell all that he had and to give it to the poor. Notwithstanding Aquinas's acceptance that "those . . . in authority rightly tolerate certain evils, lest certain goods be lost or certain greater evils be incurred", modern Catholic thinkers have tended to conflate what would be perfect in an individual with what might be desirable from a government. Rightly, we admire people who are generous to those worse-off than themselves. There is a world of moral difference, though, between an individual choosing to give something away and a government forcing people to do so, even in a good cause. When I give something away, that's charity. When the government takes from me, even for the benefit of someone worse-off, that's still coercion (even if it may sometimes be justifiable).

In my view, it's impossible to be virtuous using someone else's money, hence my discomfort with the 'social justice' (or indeed 'social gospel') advocacy that seeks punitive rates of taxation in order (say) to alleviate poverty. All we can demand of government is that it be just, not that it be charitable; and much that might be worthy in an individual, if made mandatory by government could become positively oppressive. For instance, why should a price set by a tribunal be more morally compelling than a price arrived at through the operation of markets—especially as the lived experience of price control has generally been more authoritarian governments and less prosperous economies? Hence my caution with the 'distributism' that's so frequently associated with Catholic social teaching.

Craven critiques the three broad strands of Australian politics: liberalism, he says, puts freedom on too much of a pedestal and thereby gives the strong too much of an opportunity to oppress the weak; conservatism, he says, can too readily degenerate into a rear-guard action in defence of the status quo; while social democracy, he says, entails big government making decisions that should be left to individuals and local communities. I don't think he gives enough credit to a 'Burkean conservatism' which appreciates that individuals can only be realised in a community that values the freedom that "slowly broadens down from precedent to precedent".

I suspect that quite a lot of Catholic social thinking is still focussed on *Rerum novarum* and *Quadragesimo anno* rather than on the updating of these classic encyclicals in *Centesimus annus*; which, says the American Catholic thinker, George Weigel, is the Church proposing "to the world of the twenty-first century" a "free and virtuous society . . . composed of three interlocking parts: a democratic political community, a free economy, and a robust moral culture". Weigel observes that the *Centesimus annus* teaching on the need for a free economy is still frequently lost in what he calls "the quixotic search for a 'Catholic third way' somewhere 'beyond' capitalism and socialism".

It's significant that such a champion of the church as Weigel can pose the question, of the latest 'social' encyclical, Francis's *Laudato si*, "does [it] reflect a wrestling with the full range of scientific opinion on global climate issues?" without seeking to answer it. The Pope is entirely correct to stress the importance of stewardship and to denounce wanton environmental destruction. I agree with His Holiness that everyone has a duty to protect the planet but respectfully dissent from any claim that the science of climate change is clear and the inference that reducing carbon dioxide emissions is a moral duty, especially to the extent that it imposes higher costs on the poor. As Cardinal Pell noted in his prison diary, "many in the Vatican have jumped on the climate change bandwagon despite the encyclical *Laudato si* twice acknowledging that the Church should leave the science to the scientists. It could be a mistake like the one the papacy made with Galileo."

Yet however refined and elaborated, even by the great Saint John Paul II, I'm still sceptical of the extent to which Catholic social teaching can take us from worthy principles to practical policy; unless, of course, we're prepared to defer to a social policy 'magisterium' (which I don't think Craven is proposing). Some things may be off limits for a serious Catholic in public life: such as even more permissive abortion laws or the legalisation of assisted suicide (based, it should be said, on a universally accessible conception of human dignity rather than any church diktat). Even so, the presence of serious Catholics at all points of the political compass, at least those falling between complete libertarianism and green absolutism, should be grounds for caution against any attempt to distil compelling 'Catholic' positions; although that hasn't stopped some Catholics casting moral thunderbolts against others.

In May 2014, for instance, the Australian Catholic Bishops Conference statement on asylum seekers queried whether the government's border protection policies were motivated by "latent racism" and the "selfishness of the rich" before declaring "enough of this institutionalised cruelty" and calling "on the nation as a whole to say no to the dark forces which make these policies possible". It's a little surprising that church leaders steeped in Catholic social teaching could see no moral merit whatsoever, not even a scintilla of argument for policies that had stopped people coming to Australia illegally by boat, and thereby saved the thousands of lives lost in the people-smuggling trade. This perverse insistence that the policies that had worked to stop the boats were somehow at odds with Catholic teaching brings to mind the aphorism attributed to Cardinal Newman: that when truth and Catholicism are in conflict, either it's not really true, it's not really Catholic, or there's no real conflict!

I'm with Craven in doubting that more spending is the way to improve school performance; but wouldn't discount quite as readily as he does seeking higher entry standards for student teachers. I'm with him in his insistence that the aged should not be seen as a 'burden' on society but contend that there are limits to how much can be spent, even on the most admirable objectives. Likewise on wanting some recognition for Indigenous people in the Constitution; but does this really entail the constitutional entrenchment of a new entity giving some, but not others, their own unique 'voice' to parliament? There's an important moral dimension to all these policy questions but I'm not convinced there's a uniquely Catholic perspective.

Craven is on much stronger grounds, in my judgment,

lamenting the "disconnected pragmatism" and "transactional politics" that he thinks has come to dominate our public life, where "some crisis or loss in an opinion poll" drives decision-making rather than a framework of principles. I suspect that what most changes in our public life is less the subject matter of the arguments than the human factor in politics. If our public life is now as diminished as Craven suggests, that may have more to do with the quantum of character, conviction, and courage in our current crop of leaders than the ubiquity or otherwise of Catholic social teaching. If politics is downstream of culture, the best way to improve it may be to re-kindle an appreciation of the best that's been thought and said and to encourage men and women who see public life more as a calling than a career.

Of course, every politician must want to win: the pre-selection, the seat, and the general election. The difference is between those for whom winning matters and those for whom winning is all that matters—and are, therefore, prepared to sacrifice their colleagues, their principles, and their integrity in order to succeed. It's possible to agree with Gough Whitlam that "only the impotent are pure" while regretting (with Craven) the ruthless careerism that these days seems to characterize public life. For instance, how many senior politicians are there now, on either side, ready to run serious political risks even for policy change that's urgently needed?

This, in my view, is the true vocation of the church in the world: it's less to preach politics than to encourage all men and women of goodwill, especially those labouring in the vineyard of public life, more of whom might to our general advantage be steeped in the ideals of duty and service, indeed the humility that faith helps to engender. The mission of the church is not to make us perfect but to make us better. Catholic social teaching has an important role to play in shaping our thinking and our characters but not to direct our policies. After all, can anyone point to a moral theologian who has also been an effective statesman?

2.

Opening dialogue in government, education and workplace

Philip Booth

GREG CRAVEN'S ESSAY is timely, thought-provoking, and an important contribution to our thinking about how Catholic social thought and teaching can influence the way we consider public policy issues. Indeed, the opening sentence of Craven's second paragraph raises an issue of crucial importance—that of Catholic education. An authentic understanding of Catholic social thought can help us contribute more effectively to debates in this area in a way that can benefit the whole of society and prevent the march of secular authoritarianism.

Craven mentions that Catholics are often regarded as indulging in 'special pleading' for their schools. I see that in my own country. Catholics often talk about the post-war British settlement, whereby the state funds Catholic schools, as a 'privilege' that we should defend. Indeed, it is a privilege in the proper sense of the word (that is a law to benefit a particular interest). Laws were passed that gave Anglican, Catholic and, to a more limited extent, Jewish schools the right to receive state funding whilst remaining more independent from the state than other state-funded schools. When the vast majority of the country were adherents to one of these religions, this was a reasonable position. To move to fully-state-funded education, and take taxes from Catholics, whilst not allowing parents to choose a Catholic school, would have been an injustice.

However, this settlement has come under increasing attack from secularists. Secularists wish to de-fund religious schools so that the practical reality would be that all children would have to go to non-religious schools unless their parents paid for their children to attend private schools out of their income which would have been diminished by the taxes raised to pay for state schooling. The secularists wish to impose their model of non-religious education on the whole country regardless of what parents want.

I do not believe that you can defend the current position in the long-term by 'special pleading' or by trying to hold on to a 'privilege'. However, we can use the principles of Catholic social teaching to defend it—and, indeed, to propose the extension of freedoms that parents should have.

Greg Craven discusses education at length in the later part of his paper. However, he is examining more practical problems. It is worth taking a step back and examining how Catholic social teaching can help us understand the proper role of the state in education at a more fundamental level.

The Vatican II document *Dignitatis humanae*,[1] as well as church teaching more directly related to education, demands that all families should be able to choose an education for their children in accordance with their conscience. It is worth quoting the whole of paragraph 5 of *Dignitatis humanae*:

> The family, since it is a society in its own original right, has the right freely to live its own domestic religious life under the guidance of parents. Parents, moreover, have the right to determine, in accordance with their own religious beliefs, the kind of religious education that their children are to receive. Government, in consequence, must acknowledge the right of parents to make a genuinely free choice of schools and of other means of education, and the use of this freedom of choice is not to be made a reason for imposing unjust burdens on parents, whether directly or indirectly. Besides, the right of parents are violated, if their children are forced to attend lessons or instructions which are not in agreement with their religious beliefs, or if a single system of education, from which all religious formation is excluded, is imposed upon all.

The state exists to serve the family and not the other way round. The state should not diminish the finances of the family via taxation and then require parents who want a Catholic education for their children to pay for a private education. But how do we defend this position without resorting to special pleading?

As is clear in *Dignitatis humanae*, one of the documents of the Second Vatican Council, freedom of conscience is a universal right. We cannot be fully human unless we are able to choose the good. The state should not suppress conscience. The principle of human dignity means that all parents should be able to choose an appropriate school for their children. We are not demanding for Catholics what we do not demand for others—though it is reasonable that we focus on the needs of Catholic parents. If this means the explicit state funding of humanist schools, we should not object. The practical ways in which this will be put into practice will vary from country to country and from culture to culture. However, one way is to allow freedom for those wanting to establish schools and then to fund parents to purchase an education on behalf of their child at a school of their choice.

This would also see the principle of subsidiarity at work which demands that the state should not interfere in the decisions of families and communities. Families choosing schools and groups wishing to establish schools would have the autonomy that is proper to them.

The principle of solidarity would also apply. We should remember that solidarity is a virtue to be practised by all members of society—it is not a political action plan for the state. The church should do what it can to ensure that those families of lesser means can have an education for their children. That is exactly what the church did in England in the late nineteenth century. Indeed, my university was founded as a training college for teachers who would educate the very poorest children in Catholic schools which, at that time, were not funded by the state. Solidarity may also demand that the state provides funding in various ways to families so that they can afford an education for their children. In the West, that tends to be by fully funding school places.

Through this approach, parents will have the autonomy they deserve, freedom of conscience will be promoted, and Catholic schools can become beacons of common life, as well as a preparation for the common life within their communities as they have been for centuries. At the same time, parents of other faiths would have the same freedom as Catholic parents.

Of course, the government might have to impose what should be a limited number of constraints on schools to ensure that they do, indeed, promote the common good. Girls and boys must be treated with equal dignity and schools should not promote a hostility to the state or promote violence.

In this area, the Catholic Church does do not need to ask for privileges or indulge in special pleading. And we can avoid the secular, relativist dictatorship which many humanist groups wish to impose. We can sell our message as something positive and we can use our excellent schools as examples of what can be achieved.

This example, which complements, rather than contradicts, Greg Craven's own discussion of education, shows how the application of the principles that Craven enunciates can make a really important contribution to public policy debates—and one which is widely accepted by people of goodwill who are not Catholics. You do not have to be a political philosopher or a theologian to understand the argument above about the different roles of the family, the community, schools, and the state.

There are other public policy areas to which we could apply the same reasoning. Perhaps most notable in the United Kingdom would be the area of healthcare where, more or less uniquely in the Western world, we have a nationalised system of healthcare provision entirely funded by central government, and where nearly all providers are answerable to and owned by central government. Church providers are squeezed out of the system. As it happens, the National Health Service in the United Kingdom also does not produce successful results and this has been especially notable during the Covid pandemic. Catholic social teaching would provide an excellent guide for reform along similar lines as those proposed above for education.

Even where the principles of Catholic social teaching are applied, there is still plenty of room for political debate. How much freedom should schools have? How much funding should the state provide? To what extent and how should the state control the curriculum? My answers to these questions would be "a lot", "it should not fully fund schools" and "only in very limited ways" respectively. Others of a less liberal disposition, even applying the principles of Catholic social teaching, might come up with different answers.

In the context of my commentary on Craven's essay, the most important point is that the principles of Catholic social teaching are an important point of engagement with the world. They open dialogue. Many people accept the principles as reasonable even if they have not thought about them deeply. Certainly, you do not have to be a Catholic to welcome the key tenets of Catholic social teaching.

At the same time, it is important that Catholic academics and intellectuals engage with others in a way that takes on their arguments at their strongest points. And this takes me to the earlier part of Greg Craven's essay in which he discusses various schools of political thought. One of those schools of thought is political and economic liberalism, which is that with which I am probably most closely associated.

Interestingly, one of the authors Craven cites on numerous occasions, Adrian Pabst, wrote an article recently in the *New Statesman*.[2] In that article, he tore into liberalism and took precisely the opposite of the approach of taking on the arguments of his opponents at their strongest. I should add that his article does not reflect an unwillingness by Pabst to be open to debate more generally. He kindly appointed me as a senior research fellow in the Centre for Federal Studies which he directs at the University of Kent. I am tackling the article here and not the man.

For example, Pabst writes:

> The chief promoters of market fundamentalism such as the Austrian economist Friedrich Hayek . . . Building on the body of liberal political thought by Thomas Hobbes, John Locke and John Stuart Mill, market fundamentalists reduced humans to 'homo economicus', a rational, selfish animal in search of happiness in the pleasures of cheap consumer goods and wealth accumulation.

This caricature of the Austrian school economist, F. A. Hayek, is ridiculous. *Homo economicus* is explicitly not the model of Austrian school economists. Most of the other sentiments in the paragraph are tendentious—at best. In his Nobel Prize lecture, Hayek praised the late scholastic thinkers who, in many ways, formed the bridge between the thinking of Saint Thomas Aquinas and the modern interpretation of the natural law tradition in *Rerum novarum*, the first major modern teaching document of the Catholic Church.[3] Indeed, some Austrian school academics, such as De Soto,[4] trace the roots of that school, of which Hayek is the most famous member, to those late scholastic thinkers. Though Hayek opposes the central planning of economic and social life, because he believes it to be impossible, and is in favour of general, common law principles of law enforced through courts rather than detailed prescriptive regulation of economic life developed in and enforced through regulatory bureaus, he is hardly an anarchist. His last book, *The Fatal Conceit*,[5] is partly a defence of tradition, including religion. Indeed, Hayek's main field of study was the role of the individual in society, though he did not believe in the central planning and direct organization of society by the state. As Hayek wrote:

> This fact should by itself be sufficient to refute the silliest of the common misunderstandings: the belief that individualism postulates (or bases its arguments on the assumption of) the existence of isolated or self-contained individuals, instead of starting from men whose whole nature and character is determined by their existence in society. If that were true, it would indeed have nothing to contribute to our understanding of society.[6]

What has this got to do with Greg Craven's essay? Craven might protest that he does not mention Hayek specifically. However, the danger to which I am pointing is a general one. To use labels without interpretation can close down rather than open up debates and, in the process, reduce our ability to influence others.

Craven himself begins with a critique of schools of thought which he suggests are dead ends. Like Pabst, he builds up some caricatures. Apparently, liberals are people who believe that economics should have the final say in the organization of society. Whilst that may be true of some liberals, the basic liberal position is one that believes that the organization of society should not be planned by the state. People who believe that economics should have the final say in the organization of society are utilitarian materialists and you can find such people amongst liberals and socialists.

Essentially, Craven commits a category error here. It is an error rather like accusing people who believe that the state should not interfere in the sexual lives of adults of being supporters of 'free love'. People who are highly socially conservative can believe in a limited role for the state in these areas, just as people who believe strongly in collective social action by free institutions (including the church) can believe that the state should not play a dominant role in economic and social life and would classify themselves as liberals.

Indeed, the height of economic liberalism in late nineteenth-century Britain was the height of the development of friendly societies, mutual building societies, mutual insurance companies, and other vehicles for fraternity and collective action, such as professions and trades unions. These are precisely the institutions admired in *Rerum novarum*, the first major modern teaching document of the Catholic Church. So, it is not correct to state, as Craven does, that liberals (as they are usually termed) do not affirm the inter-connectedness of human beings.

Craven is, though, astute to point out that liberals in general do not believe that there is a concept of "the true and the good" towards which society should be ordered. That is certainly true of Hayek.[7] At the same time, it is possible to believe that there is such a concept of "the true and the good" whilst believing in limited government. Also, there is much that religiously minded folk can learn from many liberals. The focus of some liberals on the implications of human ignorance for the social, political, and economic order ought to indicate common ground with Christians when it comes to the anthropological assumptions underlying economic analysis. And the focus of many liberals on non-state vehicles for social co-operation and welfare that emerge within society itself, which has been an important area of research, is also important. There are, therefore, substantial overlaps of interest between those who use Catholic social teaching as their guide and many economic liberals.

These misconceptions come from the tendency of political theorists to over-categorise in the process of imitating the methods of the physical sciences. Certainly, Pabst does that, and Craven is doing so too in his essay, though to a lesser extent and with more subtlety and some qualifications. Perhaps this tendency to over-categorise is best indicated by Craven's praising of Burke whilst criticising liberals. Burke was not only admired by Australian conservatives (and conservatives more generally). Liberals such as Hayek admire Burke too. In *The Constitution of Liberty*,[8] Hayek refers to Burke on over twenty occasions (and the Catholic peer Lord Acton on another twenty occasions). They are amongst the most cited authors in that acclaimed book on liberal political economy. In summary, my comment on this part of Greg Craven's essay is that, whilst interesting and enlightening, it is important to engage with ideas rather than categories. The landscape of political and economic thought is subtle.

I would like to end by mentioning another area of social and economic policy on which social democrats, liberals, and proponents of Catholic social teaching ought to be able to have interesting and perhaps productive discussions, as long as we do not define each other into categories that may not have anything to offer the discussion. This example helps to unite the two themes of my response to Greg Craven—agreement about the importance of Catholic social teaching combined with some disagreement about the over-categorisation of some secular schools.

Many people are concerned about the changing nature of work in the so-called 'gig economy'. Some suggest greater government regulation. By and large, economic liberals do not favour this approach. However, many economic liberals, in principle at least, see trades unions as important and free institutions in labour markets that provide protection, negotiating services and also provide welfare and legal services for their members. Some economic liberals are ambivalent about unions; some are hostile if they are given legal privileges, engage in class conflict, or assert monopoly power; but others see them as part of the sophisticated social order, in which they provide a valuable social and economic function as long as they are not given legal privileges. Social democrats, not surprisingly, also sympathise with unions, though perhaps as a complement to rather than a substitute for government regulation of labour markets.

Modern labour markets are becoming more complex for workers to navigate. It is difficult for those who are exploited or whose contracts are explicitly or implicitly broken to obtain redress. There are some similarities here with the situation in 1891, when *Rerum novarum* was written, even if working conditions are much better today.

In *Rerum novarum*, Pope Leo XIII explicitly warned about the dangers of the state being the primary vehicle for ensuring that families had sufficient[9], and spoke of the importance of benevolent societies. He further commented that "The most important of all are workingmen's unions."[10] These unions were expected to be of a rather general character and to exist in a climate of co-operation with employers rather than of conflict:

> They were the means of affording not only many advantages to the workmen, but in no small degree of promoting the advancement of art, as numerous monuments remain to bear witness. Such unions should be suited to the requirements of this our age . . . It is gratifying to know that there are actually in existence not a few associations of this nature, consisting either of workmen alone, or of workmen and employers together, but it were greatly to be desired that they should become more numerous and more efficient.[11]

Such societies had a natural right to exist[12] and should only be suppressed in exceptional circumstances. Furthermore, they should not, in general, be placed under the control of the civil law, but be allowed to flourish freely.[13] They should not be led by "secret leaders", not act against the public wellbeing or force working men to join them.[14] If necessary, Christians should form their own such associations.

This is a marvellous message for our times in the hundred and thirtieth anniversary year of *Rerum novarum*. All the principles of Catholic social thought are here. The dignity of the worker, the common good, solidarity, and subsidiarity (that is the rightful place of non-state organizations in promoting workers' rights). But it also provides a rich subject for discussion between experts in Catholic social thought, liberals, conservatives, and social democrats.

3.

Beyond principles alone

Sandie Cornish

At the heart of Professor Craven's essay is a deep concern for the ineffective and inappropriate nature of the transactional politics that has dominated Australian policymaking in recent years. This dynamic has also been evident in the national life of various other countries, including the United States of America. It is a concern addressed in detail, and at times with a startling directness, by Pope Francis in his encyclical on fraternity and social friendship, *Fratelli tutti*. For example, he says that politics can and must be "something more noble than posturing, marketing and media spin".[1] Both men seek "a better kind of politics" and are confident that Catholic social teaching has something to offer this enterprise.[2]

Professor Craven focusses on the potential of the core principles of Catholic social teaching to provide a framework for public policy in our religiously and culturally plural society. He suggests that the principles can be understood and accepted through the use of reason, floating free of their theological roots, and thus be accepted by people who do not share Catholic beliefs or positions. These principles can become an expression of shared values and commitments—a universal ethic rather than an attempt to impose Catholic teaching on other believers, atheists, and agnostics.

While it is true that the core principles of Catholic social teaching can provide a common language for conversation among diverse groups within Australian society—and internationally—around the kind of society that we want to live in, and what our policy objectives and approaches should be, there are also dangers and limitations to this "principles alone" approach.[3]

I will examine three such limitations and comment briefly on some additional ways in which Catholic social teaching might contribute to policy discussions in contemporary Australia.

What is the problem with principles alone? In a religiously and culturally diverse society, Catholics cannot impose their views on the whole community. If we are committed to a path of encounter, dialogue, and listening with an open heart, we will see value in language that enables conversation rather than erecting barriers.[4] The principles of Catholic social teaching can function in this way. However, there are dangers and limitations to focussing on the principles alone to the exclusion of the rest of the tradition. Rather than preventing us from using the principles of Catholic social teaching as Professor Craven has done, attention to these dangers and limitations may point us towards additional strategies.

First, a principles-alone approach can descend into a kind of essentialism, reducing the whole corpus of the teachings to one of its three basic elements and neglecting the potential contributions of the other two *viz* criteria for judgement and guidelines for action. Secondly, it can promote a deductive, top-down classicism that is out of step with the way in which the post-Vatican II social teachings go about critical reflection on social morality from the perspective of faith. Thirdly, such an approach may miss the importance of the epoch-making developments in Catholic social teaching under Pope Francis. These concerns point to different operative understandings of what Catholic social teaching is, and how the tradition functions. They can also help us to think about a variety of ways in which we can draw on and enflesh the tradition.

Those who focus strongly on permanent and universal principles within Catholic social teaching, understanding it as being, at its heart, a set of enduring and essential principles that are applied, or perhaps given new expression, in different historical or cultural contexts, could be said to have an essentialist understanding of Catholic social teaching. The ethical methodology of an essentialist approach is classical and deductive, beginning with the essence of the teachings—permanent and universal principles—and reasoning from them in relation to specific cases. Thus, positions on matters arising in any given society, and the proper approach to action in response, can be deduced from the application of the essential principles of Catholic social teaching to the situation in hand.

We can observe an essentialist understanding of Catholic

social teaching implicit in the practice of some contemporary Catholic organizations. Typically, their foundational documents will declare inspiration by Catholic social teaching and present a list of Catholic social teaching principles considered authoritative by the organization. The organization then seeks to 'apply' these abstract principles to the issues or situations at hand. The United States Bishops' Conference's influential list of seven key themes,[5] the Pontifical Council for Justice and Peace's articulation of four perennial principles,[6] and lists generated by other scholars to identify core principles[7] have been used in this way.[8] This approach emphasises the doctrinal core of the teachings—essential principles—to the exclusion of criteria for judgment, and guidelines for action.

By ignoring the substantive content of international and local teaching documents, such organizations miss out on the practical wisdom generated by the magisterium concerning specific issues, or situations. They may find themselves taking a different position from the magisterium without even being aware of, much less considering, positions that have developed over decades or even centuries, out of reflection on experience in a variety of contexts in dialogue with faith sources. There is an arrogance in rejecting long-standing positions of the tradition without actively considering them. Such positions could be useful contributions to policy discussions whether dialogue partners accept their theological foundations or not.

Criteria for judgement and guidelines for action are less authoritative elements of Catholic social teaching than principles for reflection because they inevitably rely on contingent judgments. They may have only local, and particular, rather than universal, validity. They may become superseded over time by new developments. So, it may be appropriate to take positions at variance from those expressed in previous teachings. However, these criteria for judgement and guidelines for action are something more than a cognitive exercise in policy analysis; they are the fruit of prayerful discernment by faith leaders as faith leaders. They provide connection to the lived witness of the Catholic community through time and space in a way that the application of abstract ideas alone cannot.

In *Evangelii gaudium*, Pope Francis says that "progress in building a people in peace, justice and fraternity depends on four principles related to constant tensions present in every social reality" and one of these is that "realities are more important than ideas".[9] He calls for a constant dialogue between realities and ideas lest they become disconnected, and he reminds us of the incarnational basis of theological ethics' 'turn to experience' in "the principle of reality, of a word already made flesh and constantly striving to take flesh anew".[10]

Today, theological ethics involves experience and change. The classicism of pre–Vatican II documents of early modern Catholic social teaching, including *Rerum novarum*, to which Professor Craven gives such great emphasis, tends towards an essentialist understanding of Catholic social teaching. The logic of the Thomistic method and anthropology adopted by Leo XIII and Pius XI can be explained in this way: "God created the world in accord with God's plan but also gave human beings reason so that, reflecting on human nature and all that God created, we can discover what God wants us to do."[11] By arguing from reason rather than from explicitly Christian sources, Leo XIII and Pius XI were able to address all people. Professor Craven sees value in doing the same today.

However, the teachings of Vatican II abandoned the notion that social issues are separate from the supernatural, and their ethical methodology shifted towards historical consciousness.[12] This is evident in the famous opening paragraph of the Pastoral Constitution on the Church in the Modern World, *Gaudium et spes*. It announces that the followers of Christ share the "joys and hopes, griefs and anxieties" of contemporary people, "especially those who are poor or in any way afflicted," because "they are led by the Holy Spirit in their journey to the kingdom of their Father and they have welcomed the news of salvation," which is meant for all and is "truly and intimately linked with [humankind] and its history."[13]

The influential, but somewhat controversial, North American moral theologian Charles Curran[14] explains that an historically conscious ethical methodology gives more weight to "the particular, the contingent, the historical, and the changing" and "induces its conclusions by examining different contingent historical situations"; therefore it "can never claim the absolute certitude of deduction; it is satisfied with moral or practical certitude."[15]

Prior to the pontificate of Francis, *Octogesima adveniens* provided the strongest expression of an historically conscious ethical approach in papal Catholic social teaching. Acknowledging the diversity of situations in which people live around the world, Paul VI concluded that it was difficult to "utter a unified message" or to offer "a solution which has universal validity" and declared that this was not his mission.[16] Paul VI advocated an inductive approach. Action is to start from the local and the particular rather than from universal and unchanging principles—each Christian community is to "analyse with objectivity the situation which is proper to their own country, to shed on it the light of the Gospel's unalterable words and to draw principles of reflection, norms of judgment and directives for action from the social teaching of the church."[17]

In *Evangelii gaudium*, Francis quotes *Octogesmia adveniens* with approval concerning the impossibility of preaching a single universally valid message in the face of widely varying contexts.[18] He calls for greater decentralisation in the church, saying: "it is not advisable for the Pope to take the place of local Bishops in the discernment of every issue which arises in their territory. In this sense, I am conscious of the need to promote a sound 'decentralization'."[19] By using the qualifier "sound" in relation to decentralisation, Francis indicates that he sees a continuing role for universal as well as local teachings.

Pope Francis's teaching has marked a shift in emphasis, expression and style in Catholic social teaching compared with his immediate predecessors. He is world-embracing and conversational. For him, the tradition evolves through dialogue between principles, context, experience, and reflection. Francis demonstrates a praxis approach to theology in *Laudato si'* by starting from experience and placing data in dialogue with faith sources for the sake of action. He draws wisdom from the tradition to respond to reality rather than deductively applying principles. *Evangelii gaudium* had flagged this approach, insisting that "realities are greater than ideas"[20] and that "there is a constant tension between ideas and realities. Realities simply are, whereas ideas are worked out. There has to be a continuous dialogue between the two, lest ideas become detached from realities."[21] Furthermore, "the principle of reality, of a word already made flesh and constantly striving to take flesh anew, is essential to evangelisation . . . this principle impels us to put the word into practice, to perform works of justice and charity which make that word fruitful."[22]

For Paul VI and for Francis, evangelisation is not just the application of the Gospel to each particular experience of life. The story of God amongst us can also be discovered and understood more deeply through examining life itself. God's ongoing action in history continues to transform personal and social relations. The dynamic at work can be described in this way: "there are eternal truths—but one does not deduce moral principles from them. Instead, human beings can find the traces of these truths and thus shed some light on their situation" and as people become better informed and educated "important moral values . . . [are] inductively realised in the course of historical development."[23]

While continuity is typically stressed by papal authors, the content of the major international Catholic social teaching documents demonstrates that the teachings do in fact develop over time.[24] Consider, for example, the fact that although subsidiarity is considered a perennial principle of Catholic social teaching, it was not articulated in a social encyclical until 1931.[25] Some developments are prompted by external stimuli such as historical events,[26] others reflect internally generated learning grounded in reflection on experience,[27] or the assimilation of ideas that originated elsewhere.[28]

Rather than focusing tightly on essential principles, many scholars today see Catholic social teaching as evolving over time in dialogue with experience and reflection. For example, Curran affirms the need to examine the local and particular while calling for some universality—global ethics are needed for a globalised world.[29] Similarly, Jesuit moral theologian Thomas Massaro suggests that the tradition renews itself by examining reality in the light of the Gospel and Christian theology, responding with creative solutions to changing realities that draw on previous insights and build on them. At the same time, "there is also a set of core principles regarding social justice and moral obligations that should shape human activity in every age."[30] Fellow Jesuit and distinguished ethicist David Hollenbach shares this approach, reconstructing such core principles as the common good in ways that speak to the contemporary situation.[31] He holds that the tradition is always *in via* or on the way to deeper understanding of revelation, and of how human beings should live together, and that it is capable of assimilating ideas originally discovered elsewhere. Furthermore, God both transcends history and is present within it—revelation continues to unfold, bringing possibilities of new insights from our discovery of God's ongoing action in the world.[32]

This understanding of Catholic social teaching as an evolving tradition can be seen in the practice of Catholic organizations that see spirituality and ethics as integrally linked in persons and communities seeking to imitate Christ.[33] They adopt approaches that explicitly draw on faith sources as well as reason. The see-judge-act model of the Cardijn movements and the pastoral spiral methodology commonly used by the Federation of Asian Bishops Conferences are two examples of such approaches. This understanding of Catholic social teaching would lead us to place not only the enduring principles of Catholic social teaching, but also its criteria for judgment, and the specific guidelines for action that universal and local social teachings may have articulated on the issue or situation, in dialogue with experience in context. Not only may core principles be given new expression, but they may also be understood more deeply, refined, and nuanced. The accumulated experience of reflection on action going back to the origins of the church contributes to the development of the teachings in the unfolding of salvation history.

New teaching may emerge in response to new situations and issues. Local action and reflection is seen as informing, as well as being informed by, international teachings.[34] Reflection on experience might then contribute to the development of teachings by: revealing gaps in teachings; prompting the refining of existing teachings; suggesting that certain teachings are not sustainable in the light of actual outcomes where a contingent judgment is not borne out in practice; making explicit what was previously implicit; offering new ways of expressing teachings or a change in emphasis among elements of existing teachings; and incorporating insights that originated elsewhere. By holding up new or previously neglected aspects of reality, and including previously excluded experiences and perspectives, we may contribute to the development of Catholic social teaching by recognising new spaces for the encounter of Scripture and tradition with reality.

None of this suggests that there is anything wrong with using core principles of Catholic social teaching to engage broad audiences in policy conversations. But it does caution us against presenting Catholic social teaching as a codified framework of unchanging principles, because this leaves no room for the incarnation, revelation, salvation, grace, or God's ongoing action in the world. Nor does it allow for the articulation of new core principles.

The third danger of an exclusive focus on the principles of Catholic social teaching that I wish to highlight is that such an approach may lead us to miss the importance of epoch-making developments in Catholic social teaching under Pope Francis. We must be sure to notice his "revolution of tenderness".

Professor Craven rightly pays attention to *Rerum novarum*. It was not, as some claim, the beginning of Catholic social teaching, but it was a landmark document. It was the first formal papal teaching document on social issues to accept modernity and it ushered in the tradition of modern Catholic social teaching. Its teachings have been revisited and further developed by a string of anniversary encyclicals. For example, John Paul II's *Laborem exercens* addresses human work in the context of major technological change, a globalising economy, and the development of the social welfare state. The only other Catholic social teaching document so far to be commemorated with anniversary encyclicals is Paul VI's *Populorum progressio*,[35] which Benedict XVI hailed as the "*Rerum novarum* of the present age".[36]

Rerum novarum, and subsequent social encyclicals, saw work as the key to the 'social question' until Paul VI's *Populorum progressio* placed the concept of integral human development at the centre. Now, Pope Francis is reframing the tradition with his teaching on care for creation and placement of integral ecology—which includes but goes beyond integral human development—at the centre. I believe that *Laudato si'*[37] will come to be seen as the third pivotal social encyclical of modern Catholic social teaching.

Professor Craven focussed on four core principles identified as perennial by both the Congregation for Education's 1989 *Guidelines on the Study and Teaching of Catholic Social Doctrine in the Formation of Priests*[38] and the Pontifical Council for Justice and Peace's 2004 *Compendium of the Social Doctrine of the Church.*[39] This choice is reasonable. It is one that I often make in introducing key ideas from the tradition. However, it seems to trouble people that there are, as we have noted, different lists of principles. I am frequently asked whether a particular list is correct or not. There is no single definitive official list of Catholic social teaching principles, because that is not how the tradition functions. The 'correct' list to use is one that accurately reflects insights from the tradition and is fit for purpose in context. We start from reality and "bring out from our treasure what is new and what is old" as John Paul II explained, referencing Mathew 13:52 in *Centesimus annus*.[40] The list of Catholic social teaching principles that are most important in the work of a development agency in Australia may not be the same as the principles that are most relevant to the work of educators in the Pacific or non-violent protest movements in Asia.

Had the *Guidelines* or the *Compendium* been written in 1959 or 1964, it seems unlikely that solidarity would have been included in the list of perennial principles, as this language was not yet common in Catholic social teaching. If new editions of these publications were produced in 2021, it seems likely that integral ecology would be recognised as a perennial principle.

What impact might the inclusion of integral ecology as a fifth perennial principle have had on Professor Craven's policy objectives and proposals?

Contemporary Catholic social teaching does not see the purpose of public policy as simply the promotion of human wellbeing. Francis challenges an arrogant anthropocentricism that rebels against the fact that we human beings are God's creatures in company with the rest of God's creation. He calls us to a renewed anthropology and cosmology. Our care for creation is not to be simply self-serving or managerial, but rather grounded in recognition of the intrinsic value of every element of creation, and our relationship of kinship as fellow creatures.[41] Francis's concept of integral ecology stresses that "everything is closely interrelated" which is why he frequently couples the cry of the earth and the cry of the poor.[42] The implications for policy discussions are legion.

Francis is also extending our understanding of existing principles that have stood the test of time.

The principle of integral ecology does not so much derive from that of human dignity as stand alongside it, affirming that all creatures speak to us of the Creator, and have an intrinsic value and worth.[43] The common good is not only to be understood as global but also intergenerational[44]—it may even embrace the good of the rest of creation.[45] Our solidarity clearly needs to embrace the whole of creation in a relationship of care and kinship, not just other human beings, as suggested so poignantly by St Francis of Assisi's Canticle of the Creatures.

Care is a key word for Francis. He has shifted the focus of Catholic social teaching from duty-based ethics to a virtue ethic of care and kinship—he invites us to join Jesus' "revolution of tenderness".[46] Our care must extend to all people and all of creation. This way of the heart takes us beyond a tight focus on the cognitive and cannot be reduced to principles or codified in comprehensive frameworks. A fully human response must integrate the cognitive, affective, effective, and volitional—uniting our hearts, heads, and hands for the mission of God.

If principles alone are not enough, or at least entail dangers and limitations, what else can the Catholic social justice tradition offer to engagement with policy problems? Three other ways in which the tradition can contribute to public policy are:

- through the articulation of vision and principles in dialogue with others;

- offering questions, critiques and suggestions grounded

in reflection on experience; and

- prophetic witness that demonstrates the possibility of alternatives.

The core principles of Catholic social teaching do not provide a comprehensive vision of how society should be organized, but they do articulate elements of such a vision in a way that can be broadly shared. The fundamental source of our Catholic vision of the good society is in the unfolding story of God's love. It is revealed in Scripture and in the ongoing action of God in the world. Catholic social teaching principles give expression to at least part of what we have learnt so far.

The majority of Australians are believers, and their religious beliefs influence their vision of the good society. Conversation at the level of faith can help to uncover and express shared commitments in a pluralist society. The Sydney Statement is just one example of the articulation of shared values and principles generated by interfaith dialogue.[47] The Sydney Statement was created by Youth PoWR (Parliament of the World's Religions), an interfaith initiative that brings young adults from different religions together to have a voice in shaping our multicultural, multi-religious society. They affirm the values of: the dignity of the human person; life; freedom; equality; safety and security; hospitality; gratitude; generosity and service; humility; respect; openness; care for the environment; and solidarity, together with the principles of: multiculturalism; citizenship; democracy; secularity; the rule of law; and the compatibility of science and religion. Each of these values and principles is consistent with Catholic teaching.

At a practical level, working from an interfaith articulation of shared values and principles can avoid the misapprehension that the Catholic Church is trying to force its preferences on the whole community. More importantly, the practice of encounter, dialogue, and seeking the good together is an expression of our own tradition's understanding of the demands of fraternity and social love and the path to peace.[48] Rather than simply drawing on our own tradition's articulation of principles, we can build up belonging and a sense of shared Australian values by engaging in these processes. We can recognise that all genuine faith reflects a spark of the Divine.

The evolving nature of our social justice tradition reminds us that we don't know it all. We cannot provide a perfect framework for policy issues that covers everything because revelation continues to unfold. We can however contribute questions grounded in faith and reflection on experience. As Professor Craven notes, asking the right questions can make a crucial difference.

Our social justice tradition is not just one of documents and ideas but also of lived witness and action. We can offer into policy discussions our experience—both successes and failures—in trying to contribute to a better world for all. Such experience will inform our questions, our critiques of policies and proposals, and our suggestions. Obviously, the Catholic Church and its organizations bring an enormous amount of experience over extended periods in Australia and elsewhere to the policy arenas of education and healthcare which Professor Craven takes up as examples.

Catholic people and organizations, especially the religious institutes and the many services that they have founded, have given expression to the Catholic social justice tradition through prophetic witness that demonstrates the possibility of alternatives. The generation and piloting of alternatives assists policymakers to open up their vision and move beyond the status quo. Such alternatives are often born of closeness to those who are disadvantaged, marginalised, or vulnerable, sharing their lives and listening to their perspectives. They are grounded in prayerful attention to discerning the action of God in and through these people and communities. Thus, while the preferential option for the poor and the earth may be considered a theme in Catholic social teaching rather than a perennial principle, it is one of the most foundational and generative commitments of the People of God through time and space.

Using Catholic social teaching principles to engage in broad conversations around policy issues is a helpful strategy that has stood the test of time in widely differing contexts. The principles of Catholic social teaching can inform policy and practice by articulating elements of a vision that can motivate action, providing a framework for the assessment of action, the determination of substantive positions, and the choice of approaches to action. Nonetheless, this approach also has limitations and entails risks for our understanding of how the tradition operates.

We have seen that there is a risk of an essentialism that overlooks other useful elements of Catholic social teaching and of the Catholic social justice tradition more broadly. A tight focus on the didactic application of those principles that have stood the test of time and are considered perennial can hinder us from engaging with Catholic social teaching as an evolving tradition in which new insights may be gained inductively. We have seen too that this approach may prevent us from noticing, giving due weight to, and taking up significant developments of Catholic social teaching under Pope Francis.

Taking a more wholistic view of Catholic social teaching, embracing its contemporary approach to theological ethics, and engaging with Francis's teaching on integral ecology, fraternity, and social friendship, opens up additional ways in which the tradition can contribute to policy discussions. Three examples are the articulation of a shared vision and principles in dialogue with others; offering questions, critiques, and suggestions grounded in reflection on experience; and demonstrating through action the possibility of alternatives.

4.

Continuing impact on a changing political agenda

Kevin Rudd

REPORTS OF THE death of Christianity in Australian public life are premature. Certainly, we hear repugnant appeals by some candidates for the votes of Christians purely on the basis of their shared identity, or equally vacuous appeals around a narrow set of political demands focussed almost exclusively on sexual morality. Often, these are cloaked in the rhetoric of 'family values' while simultaneously making life harder for these very same families by attacking their wages and conditions, withdrawing essential public goods like universal healthcare and affordable higher education, or threatening the retirement incomes of working people.

But perhaps worse still, we hear calls to 'keep religion out of politics', echoed presently by our prime minister, who professes a deep Pentecostal faith and is content to be photographed in worship at election time, but refuses to discuss publicly how his concept of Christian ethics inform his politics. It needn't be like that. As I wrote in 2006, well before becoming prime minister, the Gospel is both a *spiritual* Gospel and a *social* Gospel, and if it is a social Gospel then it is in part a *political* Gospel, because politics is the means by which society chooses to express its collective power.[1] The Gospel is in part an exhortation to social action. It doesn't provide a mathematical formula to answer all the great questions of our age. But it does offer a starting point to debate those questions within an informed Christian ethical framework which always preferences social justice, the poor, and the powerless. And that includes protecting the creation itself.

Greg Craven's essay rightly highlights four fundamental principles of Catholic social teaching: the dignity of the human person, the common good, subsidiarity, and solidarity. These are proud principles. They have often been invoked in one form or another by contending political actors in Australia whether they be liberals, social democrats, or conservatives. One does not have to be Catholic or committed to a distinctive Christian theology to be committed to them. It is, however, too harsh to conclude, as Craven does, that "Australian politics in the last thirty years has been more likely to be informed by a kind of disconnected pragmatism than by a framework of principles." Each prime minister would respond to that question differently, as I have in my own public dialogues with Greg at Australian Catholic University in 2018.[2]

Certainly, it's one thing to enunciate time-honoured

principles, while it is another to have them inform public policy and administration. I agree with Craven that "part of the genius of Catholic social teaching is its ability to hold its principles in creative tension" and this can be done without diminishing their potency. Whether liberal, social democrat, or conservative, "we would all like to see more justice, more equality, more liberty, more efficiency in Australian society." But how is this to be done?

My sense is that Craven sees the teaching of Pope John Paul II in encyclicals such as *Sollicitudo rei socialis* and *Centesimus annus,* which in turn were built on the insights of Pope Leo XIII in his 1891 encyclical *Rerum novarum,* as being the epitome of Catholic social teaching. No doubt these teachings contributed much to the time-honoured conflicts between capital and labour and between the liberty of the individual and the power of the state. In those areas, they will continue to provide useful contours for debate and dispute resolution. Perhaps it's no coincidence that the most recent of these encyclicals was published thirty years ago—and ever since Professor Craven thinks our politics has been lacking a framework of principles.

The political agenda during the last thirty years has changed, however, and is now constantly concerned with the challenges of climate change, inequality, meaningful work, and technological development, security of national borders, migration and refugee flows, Indigenous participation and recognition in the life of the nation state, and individual human rights in tension with the national interest or the claims of groups. Whether liberal, social democrat or conservative, it is possible for us to find common cause in prosecuting these deep agendas which go to the heart of what sort of nation we wish to be. But it is not to be done simply by the theologian sitting at a desk, seeking to strike the right balance, creatively resolving the tensions of the four key principles—the tensions between the individual's dignity and the common good, and between solidarity and subsidiarity.

Rather, the successful approach in modern politics is to commit to dialogue, taking the science seriously, acting on the evidence, and providing the opportunity for all those affected by prospective policies to have a place at the table of political deliberation. It is no longer a matter of popes or bishops from the sidelines laying down immutable principles and univocal responses as to how those principles are to be applied. It is critical that the foundations of the faith and the ethical imperatives to which they give rise are articulated clearly.

For me, Catholic social teaching is at its most relevant in an encyclical like Pope Francis's *Laudato si'* ('On Care for our Common Home'). It is addressed to "every person living on this planet." The document is the result of concerted dialogue of theologians and philosophers with experts in politics and various scientific disciplines. Though it contains specific chapters on theology and spirituality, it also contains chapters accessible and attractive to those who are not Catholic; those who are not Christian. The encyclical describes "the urgent challenge to protect our common home" including "a concern to bring the whole human family together to seek a sustainable and integral development."[3] Pope Francis is not prescriptive with answers on climate change. Rather, he appeals for "a new dialogue" and "a conversation which includes everyone."[4] Acknowledging that even believers can have obstructionist attitudes ranging from denial to indifference, including "nonchalant resignation or blind confidence in technical solutions," he calls for "a new and universal solidarity."

In a chapter entitled 'What is Happening to our Common Home', he outlines the practical problems and challenges confronting us, including pollution and climate change, water shortages, loss of biodiversity, decline in the quality of human life and the breakdown of society, and global inequality. This pope makes no pretence to provide the definitive answers to this conglomeration of global challenges. But this does not hold him back from issuing harsh judgments against those interests opposed to addressing these global concerns. He has a moral leadership on climate which he does not squander when he declares:

> The same mindset which stands in the way of making radical decisions to reverse the trend of global warming also stands in the way of achieving the goal of eliminating poverty. A more responsible overall approach is needed to deal with both problems: the reduction of pollution and the development of poorer countries and regions.[5]

He has the humility to concede:

> On many concrete questions, the Church has no reason to offer a definitive opinion; she knows that honest debate must be encouraged among experts, while respecting divergent views. But we need only take a frank look at the facts to see that our common home is falling into serious disrepair.[6]

As a long-time practitioner of politics, first on the national stage and now internationally, Pope Francis provides new possibilities for Catholic social teaching when, having gone to the trouble of consulting with a range of experts in a range of all relevant disciplines, he concedes that there is a variety of opinions. Never before have we read in a papal encyclical words to this effect:

> Finally, we need to acknowledge that different approaches and lines of thought have emerged regarding this situation and its possible solutions. At one extreme, we find those who doggedly uphold the myth of progress and tell us that ecological problems will solve themselves simply with the application of new technology and without any need for ethical considerations or deep change. At the other extreme are those who view men and women and all their interventions as no more than a threat, jeopardising the global ecosystem, and consequently the presence of human beings on the planet should be reduced and all forms of intervention prohibited. Viable future scenarios will have to be generated between these extremes, since there is no one path to a solution. This makes a variety of proposals possible, all capable of entering into dialogue with a view to developing comprehensive solutions.[7]

What then is to be done? Of course, the pope proposes the need for education and spirituality. But he dedicates an entire chapter of his encyclical to lines of approach and action. Dialogue is central to every one of them: dialogue in the international community, dialogue in national politics, dialogue and transparency in decision-making, dialogue between religion and science, and politics and economy in dialogue with human fulfilment. This is where Catholic social teaching provides ongoing assistance for those of us committed to taking on the big political challenges confronting the planet and every nation. Fostering dialogue across national borders, across ideological lines, and across disciplines is the key—while still for those of us from a Christian tradition anchored in the deep ethical principles of the Faith.

After the compromise at the Copenhagen climate conference in 2009 and in the light of the more substantive agreement reached at Paris in 2015, it is useful and encouraging to have the pope being prepared to state boldly and simply: "We know that technology based on the use of highly polluting fossil fuels—especially coal, but also oil and, to a lesser degree, gas—needs to be progressively replaced without delay."[8] Pope Francis is right to claim that "Politics and business have been slow to react in a way commensurate with the urgency of the challenges facing our world."[9] He continues to remind us that "Enforceable international agreements are urgently needed, since local authorities are not always capable of effective intervention."[10]

His distinctive contribution to the debate on climate change has been to continue to remind all protagonists that "The same mindset which stands in the way of making radical decisions to reverse the trend of global warming also stands in the way of achieving the goal of eliminating poverty."[11]

Not being a party-political player, the pope is neither liberal, social democrat, nor conservative. He is the custodian and exemplar of Catholic social teaching, not presuming to settle scientific questions or to replace politics, but "concerned to encourage an honest and open debate so that particular interests or ideologies will not prejudice the common good."[12] Espousing the principles of Catholic social teaching, the pope and the Holy See are well positioned to demonstrate how those principles might be applied in a variety of national contexts and in relation to a vast array of social and political questions. The principles have retained their vitality when popes and their representatives have engaged in true dialogue with experts and decision-makers and when they have provided guidance as to how the principles might be held in tension and applied in diverse areas of specialisation.

With my interest in international affairs, I am always assisted and challenged by the annual papal messages for the World Day of the Poor, the World Day of Peace, and the World Day of Migrants and Refugees and by the Pope's annual address to the Diplomatic Corps. Every pope since Paul VI in 1965 has addressed the United Nations, and every one of them has espoused strongly the need for a rules-based international order. In his 2015 address to the United Nations, Pope Francis reaffirmed the sentiments of his predecessors:

> The praiseworthy international juridical framework of the United Nations Organization and of all its activities, like any other human endeavour, can be improved, yet it remains necessary; at the same time it can be the pledge of a secure and happy future for future generations. And so it will, if the representatives of the States can set aside partisan and ideological interests, and sincerely strive to serve the common good.[13]

Since Paul VI's visit to India in 1964, every pope has travelled extensively, extolling and reflecting on the principles of Catholic social teaching made pertinent to diverse cultures and societies. In his seven years as pope, Francis has met with and addressed political, cultural, and religious leaders at home in their own countries—Brazil, Israel, Jordan, Palestine, South Korea, Albania, France, Turkey, Sri Lanka, Philippines, Bosnia and Herzegovina, Bolivia, Ecuador, Paraguay, Cuba, the United States, Kenya, Uganda, Central African Republic, Mexico, Greece, Armenia, Poland, Georgia, Azerbaijan, Sweden, Egypt, Portugal, Columbia, Myanmar, Bangladesh, Chile, Peru, Switzerland, Ireland, Estonia, Latvia, Lithuania, Panama, United Arab Emirates, Morocco, Bulgaria, North Macedonia, Romania, Mozambique, Madagascar, Mauritius, Thailand, Japan, and most recently Iraq. Back in Rome, the *Proceedings of the Pontifical Academy of Social Sciences* bring together outstanding scholars and practitioners. In all places and at all times, serious dialogue is the key. Francis has demonstrated himself to be a truly global pope.

In *Laudato si'*, Pope Francis shows his understanding of the pressures on elected politicians accountable not only to their consciences but also to their constituencies and their caucuses. Drawing us back to the principles of Catholic social teaching, the pope is able to call decision-makers to have due regard for the common good and not just the interests of their constituents, and to weigh the interests of future generations and not just those who exercise power and voice at the moment. The inability of politicians on all sides to deliver optimal outcomes on issues such as climate change and inequality warrants the sort of papal corrective which we find in *Laudato si'*:

> A politics concerned with immediate results, supported by consumerist sectors of the population, is driven to produce short-

term growth. In response to electoral interests, governments are reluctant to upset the public with measures which could affect the level of consumption or create risks for foreign investment. The myopia of power politics delays the inclusion of a far-sighted environmental agenda within the overall agenda of governments . . . True statecraft is manifest when, in difficult times, we uphold high principles and think of the long-term common good. Political powers do not find it easy to assume this duty in the work of nation-building.[14]

Those of us engaged in the parry and thrust of politics and committed to the hard work of finding answers to intractable problems which cannot be solved by nation states acting alone can profit from the pastoral reminder of a pope who speaks of civic and political love. Each of us is able to examine our consciences when we hear the pope declare:

> We must regain the conviction that we need one another, that we have a shared responsibility for others and the world, and that being good and decent are worth it. We have had enough of immorality and the mockery of ethics, goodness, faith and honesty. It is time to acknowledge that light-hearted superficiality has done us no good. When the foundations of social life are corroded, what ensues are battles over conflicting interests, new forms of violence and brutality, and obstacles to the growth of a genuine culture of care for the environment.[15]

Provided popes and their advisers remain engaged and troubled by the challenges of the age, whatever they may be, always participating in humble dialogue with experts and decision-makers, the principles of Catholic social teaching will continue to provide a framework for deliberation and action. But whenever popes and their advisers pontificate about solutions and answers comprehensible only to faithful Catholics, forgoing the dialogue with experts and decision-makers or those beyond the church, their teachings will be sterile, dry, and irrelevant to the tasks at hand. At the national level, local bishops need to play their part in hosting and fostering such dialogue. But alas, there has not been much of that in Australia these past thirty years. That might be a contributing factor to the malaise in our politics identified by Professor Craven.

Epilogue

Frank Brennan

IT'S REFRESHING TO HAVE two theologically literate and expressive ex-prime ministers from opposite parties providing reflections on Professor Greg Craven's diagnosis of Australian political problems and Catholic policy solutions. Having identified liberalism, conservatism, and social democracy as Australia's most prominent political traditions, Craven rightly notes that all three of these approaches to public policymaking have run into trouble these last thirty years when "it has become increasingly challenging to determine what principles motivate policy in Australian politics." For much of those thirty years, Greg Craven has been in the public square as a public intellectual with an unashamed Catholic bent. In that time, we have had seven prime ministers—if you count Kevin Rudd twice. And we've had three popes. The three-decade period commenced with the final years of long-term prime minister John Howard and long-term Pope John Paul II.

Craven restricts himself largely to the Catholic social teaching of John Paul II and those who went before him, especially Leo XIII with his 1891 encyclical *Rerum novarum*. He identifies four key principles of Catholic social teaching: human dignity, the common good, solidarity, and subsidiarity.

Having surveyed earlier books in this series with Tim Wilson writing on liberalism, Damien Freeman on conservatism, and Adrian Pabst on social democracy, Craven notes that transactional pragmatism has become a hallmark of our public policy these past thirty years with "a pronounced weakening in shared values and mutual obligation." Against this backdrop, he rightly asserts: "Part of the genius of Catholic social teaching, however, is its ability to hold its principles in creative tension, a capacity notably under-rated in Australian political discourse, with its obsession with 'winning' and 'losing', despite the fact that it is intrinsic to such Australian constitutional staples as responsible government and federalism."

Sandie Cornish, a long-time practitioner and teacher of Catholic social teaching, is right to complement Craven's reliance on the principles of Catholic social teaching as an aid to deductive reasoning with an emphasis on contingent judgments borne of applying the content of the teaching as both criteria for judgment and guidelines for action. She sees Catholic social teaching as an evolving tradition. In *Rerum novarum*, Leo XIII saw human labour and its rewards as the key social question. Pope Paul VI provided a new pivot in *Populorum progressio* when he focused on integral human development for all peoples on the planet. Pope Francis has provided a third pivot in *Laudato si'* with the emphasis on integral ecology demanding care for the whole planet (our common home) and care for those who are poor and on the margins of social existence.

While extolling freedom of contract and the right to private property, Pope Leo XIII in *Rerum novarum* had postulated:[1]

That right to property, therefore, which has been proved to belong naturally to individual persons, must in likewise belong to a man in his capacity of head of a family; nay, that right is all the stronger in proportion as the human person receives a wider extension in the family group. It is a most sacred law of nature that a father should provide food and all necessaries for those whom he has begotten; and, similarly, it is natural that he should wish that his children, who carry on, so to speak, and continue his personality, should be by him provided with all that is needful to enable them to keep themselves decently from want and misery amid the uncertainties of this mortal life.

In the 1907 *Harvester* case, Justice Higgins ruled out from the beginning the spurious argument that a fair and reasonable wage was what the market would bear. Not for him any neoliberal nostrum such as 'Let the market decide'. He observed, "The remuneration could safely have been left to the usual, but unequal, contest, the 'higgling of the market' for labour, with the pressure for bread on one side, and the pressure for profits on the other."[2]

Higgins said, "Fair and reasonable remuneration is a condition precedent to exemption from the duty; and the remuneration of the employee is not made to depend on the profits of the employer. If the profits are nil, the fair and reasonable remuneration must be paid; and if the profits are 100%, it must be paid."[3] This was Higgins's truly revolutionary insight: "The standard of 'fair and reasonable' must, therefore, be something else (than what the market will bear); and I cannot think of any other standard appropriate than the normal needs of the average employee, regarded as a human being living in a civilized community."[4]

Concluding his 1915 *Harvard Law Review* article looking back on the jurisprudence he had developed in the *Harvester* decision, Higgins enunciated the key principle: "Each worker must have, at the least, his essential human needs satisfied, and that among the human needs there must be included the needs of the family. Sobriety, health, efficiency, the proper rearing of the young, morality, humanity, all depend greatly on family life, and family life cannot be maintained without suitable economic conditions."[5]

In more recent times, both prime minister Bob Hawke and Justice Michael Kirby suggested that *Rerum novarum* had a major influence on the thinking of Higgins though he was not Catholic, and neither were they. Higgins was one of the Victorian delegates at the 1897-8 Federal Convention. He proposed that the Commonwealth Parliament should have power to make laws with respect to "conciliation and arbitration for the prevention and settlement of industrial disputes extending beyond the limits of any one State." This proposal was carried narrowly by 22-19. Bob Hawke claimed in a 2010 lecture that the "ground-breaking philosophy of *Rerum novarum* deeply influenced the thinking and arguments of Higgins who (with Kingston from South Australia) finally won the day."[6] Hawke claimed that "the logic, the humanity and the compassion of *Rerum novarum* sat squarely with the embryonic arguments that Higgins had used at the Sydney Convention and these were arguments, now bolstered by the intellectual and institutional weight of *Rerum novarum* that he was able to use with ultimate success at the 1898 Melbourne Convention."[7]

Marking the centenary of the *Conciliation and Arbitration Act* in 2004, Michael Kirby—proud of his own Northern Ireland Protestant roots—declared in a paper entitled *Industrial Conciliation and Arbitration in Australia—A Centenary Reflection*: "In the 1890s Higgins embraced ideas that had been propounded in 1891 by Pope Leo XIII in his encyclical *Rerum novarum*. As you will understand, it is no small thing for a person with such an Ulster background to adopt papal ideas".[8]

Leo XIII's ideas helped shaped the thinking of Australia's founding father and arbitration judge Henry Bournes Higgins whose political agitation helped shape the Australian Constitution and whose judgments gave shape to the distinctively Australian idea of a fair wage sufficient for the support of a worker's family.

Rerum novarum was written at a time of great social change brought about by the industrial revolution. Our twenty-first century is marked by equally significant change through technological advances and digital disruption. Realising the fruits of the *Harvester* judgment in these times of great change requires the articulation of and commitment to a new accord between government, business, and civil society. Implicit in this accord must be the sharing of responsibility to achieve the common good. Such an accord needs to temper the power and expectations of capital and offer business support to pursue affordable capital. In return, businesses must not be so burdened by unnecessary regulation as to undermine their capability to generate profits and employment opportunities especially for our young or low-skilled.

Governments also can no longer argue that they are mere stewards of the economy. They must play an active role in both the architecture of a new industrial paradigm and the creation and provision of opportunities for dignified employment, especially for those who have been excluded by the employment market. From *Rerum novarum* to *Harvester* and on to entrenched bipartisan ideas about workers' rights, we can discern the ripple effect of Catholic social teaching in the secular Australian pond, conceding that a papal utterance was not the only stone thrown into that pond. Philip Booth is right to affirm that "the principles of Catholic social teaching are an important point of engagement with the world. They open dialogue."

While Greg Craven argues that his own approach to novel questions about access to education, universal healthcare, and the need for an Indigenous Voice to Parliament have been informed by an application of the principles of Catholic social teaching, Tony Abbott, a practising Catholic, remains agnostic. He is "not convinced that there is a uniquely Catholic perspective" on any of these questions. He confines himself and his Catholic tradition to the formation of individuals who participate in public life without expecting to find Catholic answers to any contemporary political issue awaiting resolution. Rudd, the Anglican brought up Catholic, finds more fruit than does Abbott in the varied teachings of the popes reflecting on contemporary political challenges in the light of the tradition. For Rudd, the pope whoever he be is "neither liberal, social democrat, nor conservative. He is the custodian and exemplar of Catholic social teaching." Dialogue is all important—dialogue across national borders, across ideological lines, and across disciplines. In *Laudato si'*, Francis writes: "On many concrete questions, the Church has no reason to offer a definitive opinion; she knows that honest debate must be encouraged among experts, while respecting divergent views."[9]

The economist Ross Garnaut who authored the Rudd government's climate change review in 2008 claims: "The most rigorous, comprehensive and influential treatment of the ethics of climate change is Pope Francis's 2015 encyclical *Laudato si'*. In this work he applies Catholic, Christian and general ethical teachings and intellectual traditions to climate change."[10] Later in his book, *Superpower: Australia's Low Carbon Opportunity*, Garnaut observes: "Of more importance in the public discussion has been the clearer understanding of the importance of the non-economic values affected by climate change . . . Here the leading contribution has been by Pope Francis's *Laudato si'*."[11]

As we prepare for COP26 in Glasgow, the next United Nations' climate change conference, it's not only Catholics who will draw inspiration from the evolving Catholic social teaching coming from the pen of Pope Francis. None of us has all the answers on how to deal with the really big issues like climate change. But how good it is to be part of a universal church with a strong tradition in theology, philosophy, and the sciences. How blessed we are to have a church with a structure that allows one person, the pope, to convene the brightest minds in all relevant disciplines and to craft a response and a call to conversion, true to the tradition and attentive to the lived experience of the poorest and most marginalised people on earth. The pope no longer proclaims the last word, if ever he did. But he does set contours for fruitful dialogue. Even those who reject his teaching need to give an account of their reasoning. This too is an aid to dialogue. It might also be an aid for us as we seek a way forward on the vexed issue of constitutional recognition of Indigenous Australians.

When Pope John Paul II met with Aborigines and Torres Strait Islanders at Alice Springs in 1986, he said:

> What has been done cannot be undone. But what can now be done to remedy the deeds of yesterday must not be put off till tomorrow.
>
> The establishment of a new society for Aboriginal people cannot go forward without just and mutually recognised agreements with regard to these human problems, even though their causes lie in the past. The greatest value to be achieved by such agreements, which must be implemented without causing new injustices, is respect for the dignity and growth of the human person. And you, the Aboriginal people of this country and its cities, must show that you are actively working for your own dignity of life. On your part, you must show that you too can walk tall and command the respect which every human being expects to receive from the rest of the human family.[12]

Thirty-five years on, Greg Craven asserts, "The principles of Catholic social teaching anchor a recognition of an Indigenous voice in Australia's Constitution." Damien Freeman concedes that there was a time when he rashly dismissed out of hand the profound concern of others for the plight of Aboriginal people. Those words of Pope John Paul II about the need for just and mutually recognised agreement had fallen on deaf ears. Freeman, like Craven and me (the one who is "short on Greek verbs, long on witchetty grubs"), is now a strong advocate for the recognition of Aborigines in the Australian Constitution. We can all take heart at some of the developments which occurred after Pope John Paul II's visit to Alice Springs, including the ten-year existence of the Council for Aboriginal Reconciliation chaired by Patrick Dodson and the following twenty-year existence of Reconciliation Australia which bore fruit, abundant fruit, allowing more and more Australians proudly to lay claim to their Indigenous heritage, allowing more Australians to welcome and affirm this cultural renaissance and self-awakening, and providing the public space for the shared acknowledgment of Indigenous heritage and culture. This has been long slow work, but it is a national achievement which, despite setbacks, is on a trajectory headed in the right direction. It gained some traction through Pope John Paul II's articulation of a distinctive application of Catholic social teaching in the dust of Alice Springs.

We still have a long way to go in finding common ground for constitutional recognition. As that journey continues, we must continue our commitment to those First Nations organizations which are the privileged places for Indigenous Australians to obtain employment, as well as opportunities for leadership while delivering self-determining services to their own mob. These are the places where they can enact and embody their human dignity, the common good, solidarity, and subsidiarity.

As a nation we still need to do more in putting right the wrongs of the past to provide opportunities for education and training—the opportunities for choosing a way of life for those living in two worlds, those worlds described by the great anthropologist W. E. H. Stanner as the Dreaming and the Market. I dedicated my last book on Aboriginal rights, *No Small Change*, to a young Aboriginal man who took his own life at twenty-three years and to "others like him caught between the Dreaming and the Market."

As a nation, we need to concede that our constitutional arrangements are still inadequate given the failure of the Constitution even to mention Aborigines and Torres Strait Islanders and their history in this land, and the confusion of the key provision of the Constitution empowering the Commonwealth Parliament to make special laws affecting Indigenous Australians. That key provision was originally formulated at the nineteenth-century constitutional conventions to allow the Commonwealth Parliament to make laws with respect to "the affairs of people of any race with respect to whom it is deemed necessary to make special laws not applicable to the general community; but so that this power shall not extend to authorise legislation with respect to the aboriginal native race in Australia." Henry Bournes Higgins and his fellow constitutional founders envisaged that such laws would restrict unwelcome migrants like the Afghans and the Chinese. Australia's first prime minister Edmund Barton told the 1898 constitutional convention in Melbourne: "I entertain a strong opinion that the moment the Commonwealth obtains any legislative power at all it should have the power to regulate the affairs of the people of coloured or inferior races who are in the Commonwealth."[13]

In 1967 we voted overwhelmingly to extend the operation of this racist provision to include the possibility that the Commonwealth Parliament could legislate with respect to the First Australians. As judges of the High Court have said, the amended provision "was an affirmation of the will of the Australian people that the odious policies of oppression and neglect of Aboriginal citizens were to be at an end"[14] and "to mitigate the effects of past barbarism".[15] Incidentally, both those judges were Catholic. The primary object of the power as amended to include Aborigines was beneficial, removing the fetter upon the legislative competence of the Commonwealth Parliament to pass necessary laws for the benefit of Aborigines.

Surely such special laws should be passed by our Parliament only if the citizens covered by those laws seek them or agree to them. How is that to be done? To answer that question and to place the answer in the Constitution, we need to work for agreement between the major political parties and with Indigenous leaders. Until such agreement is reached, we will not get to the first step amending our Constitution. Let's remember that no one under seventy-five years of age voted in the 1967 referendum. No one under sixty-two years of age has ever voted in a successful referendum.

For his part, Tony Abbott is open to some recognition of Indigenous people in the Constitution, but asks: "does this really entail the constitutional entrenchment of a new entity giving some, but not others, their own unique 'voice' to parliament? There's an important moral dimension to all these policy questions but I'm not convinced there's a uniquely Catholic perspective." Four years ago, Aborigines and Torres Strait Islanders from the length and breadth of the country gathered at Uluru and published their Statement from the Heart calling for "the establishment of a First Nations Voice enshrined in the Constitution."

Senator Andrew Bragg is one of a new breed of federal politicians who has a commitment to Aboriginal rights across party lines and beyond the old contours of debate. He has just published his book, *Buraadja: the liberal case for national reconciliation*. Senator Bragg has been impressed by the plea of Chris Sarra, who chaired the Turnbull government's Indigenous Advisory Council, that governments stop doing things *to* Indigenous people and start doing things *with* them.[16] When Sarra retired from the Council, he said, "We shifted from the rhetoric of doing things to Indigenous people to a strength-based approach and doing things with people."[17]

Bragg confronts the difficulty of achieving constitutional reform in Australia, knowing that his Liberal Party has been much more successful than the Labor Party amending the Constitution. We've had only eight successful referenda out of forty-four attempts in 120 years. Change doesn't come unless all major political parties are on board. When it comes to any constitutional change related to Indigenous recognition, Bragg acknowledges: "Ultimately, the drafting of the constitutional amendment needs to ensure that the Constitution requires consultation with Indigenous people."[18] How is this to be done when it comes to the Uluru demand for "the establishment of a First Nations Voice enshrined in the Constitution"?

Bragg writes: "An amendment for a detailed body that is set out in the Constitution has no chance of being passed at a referendum."[19] He favours the "setting out [of] an obligation to consult with Aboriginal and Torres Strait Islander people" together with the establishment of the Voice by legislation.[20] He concludes, "It may well be the case that the only way to get a Voice up and running—and guaranteed in the Constitution—is through a gradual approach."[21]

Aboriginal leaders like Professor Megan Davis who played a key role at Uluru say that "if you legislate, it's like a pinprick in a balloon; you will deflate entirely the constitutional recognition momentum." Professor Davis is adamant: "The idea that you can just road test this for five years and all of a sudden go to referendum is simply not true. If the body is successful, there is no government that is going to want to enshrine something that keeps it accountable. If the body is not successful, then people simply won't see any point to enshrining a Voice in the Constitution. There is no good logic for legislating first."[22]

The road ahead to constitutional recognition is long, winding, and fog bound. What's essential is that intelligent committed actors of good will work co-operatively for a strength-based approach, trusting each other and doing things together. We would do well to remember Philip Booth's caution that "it is important to engage with ideas rather than categories. The landscape of political thought is subtle." Along the political and philosophical spectrum, those like Professor Davis and Senator Bragg will have distinctive contributions to make to the public discourse. Davis will have a better sense of what her people want; Bragg will have a better sense of what his political colleagues will agree to. Trusting dialogue within agreed contours is essential. This requires individuals well-formed in the art of politics developing and working with ideas which cohere not just as principles, but also as criteria for judgment and guidelines for action. The suffering and dispossession of the past might then be a shadow from the light of a future national life in which the First Australians will always be assured a place at the table of deliberation when laws and policies affecting them distinctively are contemplated or made. This would be a distinctively Australian instance of policies, laws, and constitutional arrangements posited on human dignity, the common good, subsidiarity, and solidarity. Many of us who vote for such a proposal will be able to find resonance and guidance in the principles of Catholic social teaching.

Contributors

The Honourable **Tony Abbott** AC served as the twenty-eighth prime minister of Australia.

Philip Booth is a professor of finance, public policy and ethics at St Mary's University, Twickenham.

The Reverend **Frank Brennan** SJ AO is the rector of Newman College within the University of Melbourne and a fellow of the PM Glynn Institute at Australian Catholic University.

Sandie Cornish is the social justice officer at the Australian Catholic Bishops Conference.

Damien Freeman is an advisor at the PM Glynn Institute at Australian Catholic University and general editor of the Kapunda Press.

The Honourable **Kevin Rudd** AC served as the twenty-sixth prime minister of Australia.

Notes

Introduction

1   Peta Goldburg, "Catholic Social Teaching" in Jim Gleeson and Peta Goldburg (eds), *Faith-Based Identity and Curriculum in Catholic Schools* (Routledge, 2020), pp. 31-62, p. 31.

2   Congregation for Catholic Education, *Educating to fraternal humanism: Building a civilization of love fifty years after Populorum progression* (2017), para 20–21, see: <http://www.vatican.va/roman_curia/congregations/ccatheduc/documents/rc_con_ccatheduc_doc_20170416_educare-umanesimo-solidale_en.html>.

Australian political problems and Catholic policy solutions

1   At this time, the most prominent radical approach to social and political thought in Western society was liberalism. It emphasised individual liberty in all aspects of public policy and economic initiative. Liberalism, especially the liberal individualism and *laissez-faire* capitalism that was prominent in the nineteenth century, insisted on minimal state interference in financial affairs and the relations between the owners of capital and labour (which later gave way to some extent to the social liberalism of the late nineteenth and early twentieth centuries, epitomised by the laying of the foundations of the welfare state in the United Kingdom by the Asquith Liberal government in the years before World War I). Liberalism prioritised removing state constraints on the individual and affirming private property rights, private initiative, and the role of market competition to determine prices and wage rates. At around the same time that liberalism was gaining prominence in Western societies, collectivist and socialist ideologies were also growing in popularity. Emerging in the Enlightenment thinking of the previous century, and gaining momentum in the nineteenth century with the writings of Karl Marx, there were growing political and social bodies calling for the collective ownership of property and expanding the role of the state to regulate economic and social activity. Socialism, as it was in the nineteenth century, emphasised the inevitability of class conflict between workers and employers and sought to achieve economic and social equality between all members of society through state intervention. These new movements for change were resisted by reactionary forces, typically drawn from the aristocracy, who advocated for the preservation of the status quo. Conservatives tended to remain supportive of established monarchies and institutions and traditional social norms. However, by the end of the nineteenth century, the conservatives had adopted much of liberal economic thought into their tradition, even though they remained sceptical of political and social forces for change.

Conservatives were mainly concerned with the potential for violence from liberal and socialist radicals, especially following the French Revolution and the revolutions of 1848, and the threat that they posed to a peaceful order and a stable society where people could pursue their own ends cooperatively.

2 Since the time of Charlemagne, a thousand years earlier, Catholic thinking about political authority and the church's relationship to it revolved around the monarchical structures of Europe. As a result, the church was reticent to engage with new systems of thought which challenged the existing regimes. The French Revolution, with its violent anticlericalism and hatred of Christianity, particularly hardened Catholic leadership against the new systems of political thought. The pontiff at the time of the revolution, Pius VI, who was later arrested and deported by French troops to become effectively a hostage of Napoleon, warned in an encyclical to "Beware of lending your ears to the treacherous speech of the philosophy of this age which leads to death." This statement reveals the prevailing attitude of the Vatican to liberal and socialist ideas for the century after the French Revolution. For example, Leo's predecessor, Pius IX, strongly condemned 'modernism' in his 1864 encyclical *Quanta cura*, to which he attached a *Syllabus of Errors* that condemned the position that "The Roman Pontiff can, and ought to, reconcile himself, and come to terms with progress, liberalism and modern civilisation.": Pius IX, *Syllabus errorum* (8 December, 1864), n. 80.

3 The encyclicals that followed *Rerum novarum*, often published on a noteworthy anniversary of Leo's encyclical, continued to expand the critical principles of his social teaching and apply them to the issues of their time. For example, in the light of the rise of the totalitarian dictatorships and the concentration of wealth following the Great Depression, Pope Pius XI propagated *Quadragesimo anno* in 1931. This encyclical emphasised the importance of the free formation of associations apart from the state as well as the social function of private property. For Pius, it had become clear that Catholic teaching on the 'new things' in society also had to encompass the new imposition of communist and fascist regimes, in addition to Leo's criticisms of liberalism and socialism. Thus, in the 1937 encyclicals, *Mit brennender sorge* and *Divini redemptoris*, he would issue direct condemnations of the fascist and communist dictatorships of his time. The following pontificates continued to publish contributions to the growing corpus of papal teaching on social issues. John XXIII, in his encyclicals *Mater et magistra* (1961) and *Pacem in terris* (1963) responded to growing global conflict by highlighting the disparity of wealth between different countries. As a result, he emphasised the need for justice and the pursuit of peace in foreign and international policy. John XXIII also called for greater socialisation, by which he meant insisting on economic growth that promoted the dignity of the worker, greater cooperation within society, and more equitable distribution of wealth. The Second Vatican Council pastoral constitution, *Gaudium et spes* (1965), sought to reaffirm the Catholic principle of the dignity of the individual hu-

man person and the church's solidarity with the poor. This document, in addition to the conciliar declaration *Dignitatis humanae* (1965) that affirmed the right to religious freedom, came as a reaffirmation of Catholic anthropology which sees the organisation of society as being directed to the good of the human person and the communities in which they live. Paul VI also contributed to Catholic social teaching with his encyclical *Populorum progessio* (1967) that highlights the good of the development of humanity towards more humane conditions and the development of solidarity between human beings. He continued with the Apostolic Letter *Octogesima adveniens* (1971) that responded to the development of what we would now call post-industrial society and the growth of urbanisation by calling Catholics and people of good will to aspire to greater human equality and participation. The encyclicals of John Paul II also made major contributions to the social teaching of the church with his encyclicals *Laborem exercens* (1981), *Sollicitudo rei socialis* (1987) and *Censtesimus annus* (1991), in which he highlights the recognition of the dignity of the human person and their labours as the fundamental focus of society while also reaffirming the importance of solidarity and social charity. His teachings about how we should understand politics, democracy, justice and the economy are particularly significant. The social teaching of the last century was summarised in the *Compendium of the Social Doctrine of the Church* in 2004 and has continued to be elaborated upon by Pope Benedict XVI's encyclical on Christian love, *Caritas in veritate* (2009) and Pope Francis' encyclicals on environmental justice (*Laudato si'*, 2015) and social friendship (*Fratelli tutti*, 2020).

4   The vision entailed distributing ownership of capital and productive assets more broadly and thus enabling autonomy from both state and corporate control. Following also from the examples of the worker collectives and friendly societies of in Northern England, the distributists sought to organize society through the establishment of worker-controlled cooperatives and local independent communities. Distributism introduced the possibility of systematising the fundamental principles of Catholic social teaching and applying them to contemporary political and social contexts. As a result, discussion of the 'common good', 'subsidiarity' and 'solidarity' began to move beyond being features of a religious statement just for Catholics into a system of political thought that was potentially applicable to the political, economic, and social situations in primarily non-Catholic countries.

5   Race Matthews, *Of Labour and Liberty: Distributism in Victoria 1891-1966* (University of Notre Dame Press, 2018). Matthews has published a number of scholarly works recognising distributism's significance to Australian history and its potential application for contemporary Australian public policy-making.

6   Leo XIII, *Rerum novarum*, (1891), n. 46.

7   John XXIII, *Pacem in terris,* (1963), n. 1.

8 Catholic social teaching is part of the moral teaching of the church, and Catholics recognise Catholic moral teaching as an indivisible whole, with principles that cannot be preferenced over others or ignored. The influence of Catholic social teaching primarily concerns the church's vision for how societies should be organized so that people can live lives characterised by the pursuit of the common good. The social teaching of the Catholic Church also speaks to the social implications of moral issues such as abortion, euthanasia and marriage, but this essay is focused on its foundational elements and how these apply to political and structural considerations for society, and questions of policy about them.

9 Second Vatican Council, *Gaudium et spes* (1965), n. 25.

10 Ibid., n. 26.

11 John Paul II, *Sollicitudo rei socialis* (1987), n. 38.

12 Tim Wilson, *The New Social Contract*, (Kapunda Press, 2020), n. 78.

13 Leo XIII, *Rerum novarum*, n. 54.

14 Damien Freeman, *Abbott's Right*, (Melbourne University Press, 2017), n. 7.

15 Tony Abbott, 'Beyond the Welfare State, Into Humane Services', *The Australian*, 22 November 2000. (article based on an address to the Wesley Employment Conference, 17 November 2000); Freeman, *Abbott's Right*, p. 111.

16 Freeman, *Abbott's Right*, p. 78.

17 Michael Quinlan, "Just what is the conservative idea?", National Civic Council, 18 November 2017, see: <https://ncc.org.au/>.

18 Adrian Pabst, *Story of Our Country* (Kapunda Press, 2019), p. 57.

19 Paul Keating, "When the Government Changes, the Country Changes", National Press Club, Canberra, 29 February 1996, quoted in T. Bramston (ed.) *For the True Believers: Great Labor Speeches that Changed History*, (Federation Press, 2013), p. 104.

20 John Paul II, *Centesimus annus* (1991), §49.

21 Frank Bongiorno, "The continuing story of 'our' party", *Inside Story*, 10 November 2019, see: <https://insidestory.org.au/the-continuing-story-of-our-party/>.

22 Benedict XVI, *Deus caritas est* (2005), n. 28.

23 Stephen Duckett, "Morrison's health handout is bad policy (but might be good politics)," *The Conversation*, 14 December 2018, see: <https://theconversation.com/morrisons-health-handout-is-bad-policy-but-might-be-good-politics-108747>.

24 Commonwealth, Royal Commission into Aged Care Quality and Safety, Interim Report (2020) vol. 1, p. 114.

1. Teaching for best selves not best governments
No notes.

2. Opening dialogue in government, education and the workplace

1. Second Vatican Council, *Dignitatis humanae* (1965).
2. Adrian Pabst and Ron Ivey, "Why we must build a new civic covenant", *New Statesman*, 7 April 2021.
3. It may be worth noting that Hayek received the sacraments of the Church before he died, though he was not conscious.
4. J. De Soto, *The Austrian School* (Edward Elgar, 2008).
5. F. A. Hayek, *The Fatal Conceit* (University of Chicago Press, 1988).
6. F. A. Hayek, *Individualism and Economic Order* (University of Chicago Press, 1948), p. 6.
7. See P. M. Booth and M. Petersen, "Catholic social teaching and Hayek's critique of social justice", *Logos: A Journal of Catholic Thought and Culture*, Vol. 23(1), 2020.
8. F. A. Hayek, *The Constitution of Liberty* (University of Chicago Press, 1960).
9. Leo XIII, *Rerum novarum* (1891), nn. 45-47.
10. *Ibid.*, n. 49.
11. *Ibid.*
12. *Ibid.*, n. 51.
13. *Ibid.*, n. 53.
14. *Ibid.*, n. 54.

3. Beyond principles alone

1. Francis, *Fratelli tutti* (2020), n. 197.
2. *Ibid.* The whole of chapter 5, which is titled 'A Better Kind of Politics', explores this situation and the following three chapters flesh out the kinds of responses Pope Francis advocates.
3. Bernard Brady, *Essential Catholic Social Thought*, 2nd edn (Orbis, 2017), pp. 8-9.
4. Francis, *Fratelli tutti*, See chapter six.
5. United States Catholic Bishops' Conference, "Sharing Catholic Social Teaching: Challenges and Directions", 1998, see: <http://www.usccb.org/beliefs-and-teachings/what-webelieve/catholic-social-teaching/sharing-catholic-social-teaching-challenges-and-directions.cfm> and <http://www.usccb.org/beliefs-and-teachings/what-we-believe/catholic-social-teaching/seven-themes-of-catholic-social-teaching.cfm>.
6. Pontifical Council for Justice and Peace, *Compendium of the Social Doctrine*

of the Church (St Pauls Publications, 2005), n. 160. The Pontifical Council's functions have now been subsumed into that of the Dicastery for the Promotion of Integral Human Development, established in 2017.

[7] E.g., nine key themes are listed in Thomas Massaro, *Living Justice* (Rowman and Littlefield Publishers, 2008), pp. 79–117.

[8] When the author took up the position of National Executive Officer of the Australian Catholic Social Justice Council in 1997, she inherited an operational plan that listed principles of Catholic social teaching together with strategies to enact them.

[9] Francis, *Evangelii gaudium*, (2013), nn. 221- 237.

[10] *Ibid.*, n. 233.

[11] Charles Curran, *Catholic Social Teaching 1891–Present: A historical, theological and ethical analysis* (Georgetown University Press, 2002), p. 25.

[12] *Ibid.*, p. 58. Curran notes that it was Lonergan who first explained the shift in ethical methodology in this way.

[13] Vatican Council II, *Gaudium et spes* (1965), n. 1.

[14] Fr Charles Curran's licence to teach Catholic theology was withdrawn in 1986 because of some of his positions concerning sexual morality. His research on Catholic social teaching remains widely respected.

[15] Curran, pp. 54–55.

[16] Paul VI, *Octogesima adveniens*, (1971), n. 4.

[17] *Ibid.*, n. 4.

[18] Francis, *Evangelii gaudium*, n. 184, citing *Octogesima adveniens*, n. 4.

[19] *Ibid.*, n. 16. He does however go on to "present some guidelines which can encourage and guide the whole Church in a new phase of evangelization" in n. 17.

[20] *Ibid.*, n. 233.

[21] *Ibid.*, n. 231.

[22] *Ibid.*, n. 233.

[23] Curran, p. 61.

[24] John Aloysius Coleman, "Development of Church Social Teaching", in Curran and McCormick, *Readings in Moral Theology No. 5* (Paulist, 1986), pp. 169–87. Chronological presentations by other scholars and the Pontifical Council for Justice and Peace, *Compendium of the Social Doctrine of the Church*, pp. 44–54, also demonstrate this point.

[25] Pius XI, *Quadragesimo anno*, (1931), n. 79.

[26] E.g., Leo XIII, *Rerum novarum,* (1891), responded to the plight of industrial workers following the introduction of wage labour.

[27] E.g., Pius XII learnt from the difference between Pius XI's hopes and actual experience, and moved away from the corporatist, 'third way' elements of

Quadragesimo anno, nn. 78–80.

[28] E.g., John XXIII, *Pacem in terris* (1963), refined the just war criteria in the light of the development of weapons of mass destruction and affirmed a range of human rights. *Pacem in terris*, nn. 11–27.

[29] Curran, p. 55.

[30] Massaro, p. 48.

[31] David Hollenbach, *The Common Good and Christian Ethics* (Cambridge University Press, 2002), p. xiv.

[32] David Hollenbach, *The Global Face of Public Faith: Politics, Human Rights, and Christian Ethics* (Georgetown University Press, 2003), pp. 19–38.

[33] Seamus Murphy, "Two Challenges for Social Spirituality", in *Windows on Social Spirituality*, ed. Jesuit Centre for Faith and Justice (Columba, 2003), pp. 149–50.

[34] Herve Carrier, *The Social Doctrine of the Church Revisited* (Pontifical Council for Justice and Peace, 1990), p. 14.

[35] Paul VI, *Populorum progressio* (1967).

[36] Benedict XVI, *Caritas in veritate* (2009), n. 8. As Benedict XVI notes, John Paul II commemorated *Populorum progressio* with *Sollicitudo rei socialis*, and *Caritas in veritate* was itself another anniversary encyclical.

[37] Francis, *Laudato si'* (2015).

[38] Congregation for Catholic Education, *Guidelines for the Study and Teaching of the Church's Social Doctrine in the Formation of Priests* (St Paul, 1989), pp. 51–87.

[39] Pontifical Council for Justice and Peace, *Compendium*, nn. 160–61.

[40] John Paul II, *Centesimus annus* (1991), n. 3.

[41] Francis, *Laudato si'*, n. 82-84.

[42] *Ibid.*, n. 49, n. 137.

[43] *Ibid.*, n. 221.

[44] *Ibid.*, nn. 159-160.

[45] Francis, Address to the United Nations General Assembly, 25 September 2015, see: <https://papalvisit.americamedia.org/2015/09/25/full-text-of-pope-francis-address-to-the-united-nations/>. Francis affirmed a "right of the environment" which suggests that the interests of creation may need to be included in deliberations of the common good.

[46] Francis, *Evangelii gaudium*, n. 88.

[47] See: <https://www.thesydneystatement.org.au/>.

[48] Francis, *Laudato si'*.

4. Continuing impact on a changing political agenda

1. K. Rudd, "Faith in Politics", *The Monthly*, October 2006.
2. Australian Catholic University, In conversation with Kevin Rudd and Greg Craven, 16 February 2018, see: <https://youtu.be/PAPxwBj3VOo>.
3. Francis, *Laudato si'* (2015), n. 13.
4. *Ibid.*, n. 14.
5. *Ibid.*, n. 175.
6. *Ibid.*, n. 61.
7. *Ibid.*, n. 60.
8. *Ibid.*, n. 175.
9. *Ibid.*
10. *Ibid.*, n. 173.
11. *Ibid.*, n. 175.
12. *Ibid.*, n. 188.
13. Francis, *Address to the United Nations*, 25 September 2015, see: <http://www.vatican.va/content/francesco/en/speeches/2015/september/documents/papa-francesco_20150925_onu-visita.html>.
14. Francis, *Laudato si'*, n. 178.
15. *Ibid.*, n. 229.

Epilogue

1. Leo XIII, *Rerum novarum*, n. 13.
2. *Ex Parte H V McKay* (1907) 2 CAR 1 at 3.
3. *Ibid.*, p. 5.
4. *Ibid.*, p. 3.
5. Henry Bournes Higgins, "A New Province for Law and Order: Industrial Peace through Minimum Wage and Arbitration", *Harvard Law Review*, Vol. 29(1), 1915, p. 13ff, pp. 38-39.
6. R. J. L. Hawke, Inaugural Bishop Manning Lecture, 7 October 2010, see: <https://ap01-a.alma.exlibrisgroup.com/view/delivery/61USOUTHAUS_INST/12142160220001831>.
7. *Ibid.*, p. 5.
8. M. D. Kirby, "Industrial Conciliation and Arbitration in Australia—A Centenary Reflection", 22 October 2004, see: <https://www.hcourt.gov.au/assets/publications/speeches/former-justices/kirbyj/kirbyj_22oct04.html>.
9. Francis, *Laudato si'*, n. 61.
10. Ross Garnaut, *Superpower: Australia's Low Carbon Opportunity* (La Trobe University Press, 2019), p. 23.

11 *Ibid.*, pp. 48-49.

12 John Paul II, Address to Aborigines and Torres Strait Islanders, Alice Springs, 29 November 1986, paragraphs 10-11, see: <https://www.vatican.va/content/john-paul-ii/en/speeches/1986/november/documents/hf_jp-ii_spe_19861129_aborigeni-alice-springs-australia.html>.

13 Edmund Barton, *Official Report of the National Australasian Convention Debates* (Third Session): Melbourne 1898, pp. 228-229.

14 Justice Brennan in *The Commonwealth* v *Tasmania (The Tasmanian Dam Case)* (1983) 158 CLR 1 at 242.

15 Justice Deane in *The Commonwealth* v *Tasmania (The Tasmanian Dam Case)* (1983) 158 CLR 1 at 273.

16 Andrew Bragg, *Buraadja: the liberal case for national reconciliation* (Kapunda Press, 2021), p. 86.

17 See <https://www.abc.net.au/news/2018-06-28/prime-minister-indigenous-adviser-chris-sarra-resigns/9919920>.

18 Bragg, p. 167.

19 *Ibid.*, p. 168.

20 *Ibid.*

21 *Ibid.*, p. 171.

22 ABC, Law Report, 29 June 2021, see: <https://www.abc.net.au/radionational/programs/lawreport/overwhelming-support-for-indigenous-voice-in-constitution/13401840>.

Index

Abbott, A. J. 6, 8-10, 32, 111, 116, 121
Acton, John Emerich Edward Dalberg-Acton, Lord 76
Aquinas, Saint Thomas 61 74

Barton, Sir Edmund 120
Belloc, Hilaire 18
Benedict XVI, Pope
    Caritas in veritate (2009) 92, 129
    Deus caritas est (2005) 41-42
Birmingham, Simon 45
Bongiorno, Frank 37
Booth, Philip 10, 116, 123
Bragg, Andrew 122-24
Brennan, Frank 1-2, 10
Brennan, Sir Gerard 1
Burke, Edmund 6, 31, 33, 62, 76

Casey, Michael 5
Charlemagne 128
Chesterton, G. K. 18
Cornish, Sandie 9-10, 112
Craven, Greg
    approach to Catholic social teaching 59, 72, 81-82, 85-86, 91-92, 96, 101, 109, 111-12
    biography 4-5
    critique of Australian politics 62, 64-65, 73-77, 100, 112, 116
    education policy 67-68, 71
    Indigenous affairs policy 118-19
Curran, Charles 86, 89

Davis, Megan 123-24
Deakin, Alfred 31
Dodson, Patrick 119
Donnelly, Kevin 46
Duckett, Stephen 50

Fahey, Glenn 45
Francis of Assisi, Saint 94
Francis, Pope 83, 91, 98, 106-07
    Evangelii gaudium (2013) 85, 87-88
    Fratelli tutti (2020) 81, 129
    Laudato si' (2015) 9, 62-63, 87, 92-94, 102-05, 107, 112, 117, 129
Fraser, Malcolm, 31, 33
Freeman, Damien 27, 31-34, 39-40, 112, 118-19

Galileo Galilei 63
Garnaut, Ross 117
Glasman, Maurice, Lord 14
Goldburg, Peta 3
Goss, Peter 45

Hawke, R. J. L. 114
Hayek, F. A. 73-74, 76
Hewett, Jennifer 45
Higgins, H. B 19, 113-15, 120
Hobbes, Thomas 73

Hollenbach, David 89
Howard, J. W. 53, 111
Hunter, Nolan 53

Jesus Christ 2, 60, 86, 90, 94
John Paul II, Pope Saint 63, 111, 118-19
    Centesimus annus (1991) 9, 36, 62, 93, 101, 129
    Laborem exercens (1981) 91, 129
    Sollicitudo rei socialis (1987) 25, 101, 129
John XXIII, Pope
    Mater et magistra (1961) 128
    Pacem in terris (1963) 20, 128

Keating, P. J. 35
Kingston, Charles 114
Kirby, M. D. 114-15

Leo XIII, Pope 86
    Rerum Novarum (1891) 8, 16-19, 22, 27, 30, 35, 44, 51, 62, 74-75, 78-79, 85, 91-92, 101, 111-12, 114-16, 128

Marx, Karl 35, 127
Massaro, Thomas 89
Matthews, Race 18
Meagher, Ellen 2
Meagher, R. P. 1-2
Menzies, R. G. 31
Mill, J. S. 73
Morrison, Scott 50, 99

Napoleon I, Emperor 128
Newman, Saint John Henry Cardinal 64

Pabst, Adrian, 5, 7, 27, 35, 37, 40, 73, 75-76, 112
Paul VI, Pope 87-88, 106, 128
    Octogesima adveniens (1971) 86-87, 129
    Populorum progressio (1967) 92, 112, 129
Pell, George Cardinal 63
Pius IX
    Quanta cura (1864) 128
Pius XI, Pope 85-86
    Divini redemptoris (1937) 128
    Mit brennender sorge (1937) 128
    Quadragesimo anno (1931) 62

Quinlan, Michael 34

Rudd, Kevin 9-10, 45, 111, 116
Russell, Lesley 50

Santamaria, B. A. 18
Sarra, Chris 122
Second Vatican Council
    Dignitatis humanae (1965) 69, 128
    Gaudium et spes (1965) 22-23, 86, 129
Soto, J. S. de 74
Spigelman, J. J. 1
Stanner, W. E. H. 120

Turnbull, M. B. 45, 122

Weigel, George 62
Whitlam, E. G. 18, 65
Wilson, Tim 5, 7, 27-31, 40, 112
Winterton, George 1

THE KAPUNDA PRESS
an imprint of Connor Court Publishing in association with the PM Glynn Institute

GENERAL EDITOR
Damien Freeman
PM Glynn Institute
Australian Catholic University

2021
BURAADJA
THE LIBERAL CASE FOR NATIONAL RECONCILIATION

Andrew Bragg

2020
FAITH'S PLACE
DEMOCRACY IN A RELIGIOUS WORLD

Bryan S. Turner – Damien Freeman

Dean Smith – Luke Gosling – Ursula Stephens – Jocelyne Cesari
Jim Franklin – Robert Hefner – Riaz Hassan – David Saperstein
M. A. Casey

THE NEW SOCIAL CONTRACT
RENEWING THE LIBERAL VISION FOR AUSTRALIA

Tim Wilson

TRIBALISM'S TROUBLES
RESPONDING TO ROWAN WILLIAMS

Damien Freeman

Rowan Williams – Ethan Westwood – M. A. Casey – Cristina Gomez
Nigel Zimmermann – Annette Pierdziwol – Kerry Pinkstone
Amanda Stoker – Scott Stephens – Ben Etherington – Anthony Ekpo
Austin Wyatt – Sandra Jones

2019

STORY OF OUR COUNTRY
LABOR'S VISION FOR AUSTRALIA

Adrian Pabst

THE MARKET'S MORALS
RESPONDING TO JESSE NORMAN

Damien Freeman

Jesse Norman – Marc Stears – Greg Melleuish – Adrian Pabst
Amanda Walsh – Parnell McGuinness – Michael Easson – David Corbett
Tom Switzer – Cris Abbu – Tanya Aspland – Leanne Smith – M. A. Casey

NONSENSE ON STILTS
RESCUING HUMAN RIGHTS IN AUSTRALIA

Damien Freeman – Catherine Renshaw

M. A. Casey – Nicholas Aroney – Emma Dawson
Terri Butler – Jennifer Cook – Bryan Turner – Tim Wilson

FEDERATION'S MAN OF LETTERS
PATRICK MCMAHON GLYNN

Anne Henderson

Anne Twomey – Suzanne Rutland – Patrick Mullins – John Fahey
Peter Boyce

2018

TODAY'S TYRANTS
RESPONDING TO DYSON HEYDON

Damien Freeman

J. D. Heydon – Frank Brennan – Anne Henderson – Paul Kelly
M. A. Casey – Peter Kurti – M. J. Crennan – Hayden Ramsay
Shireen Morris – Michael Ondaatje – Sandra Lynch – Catherine Renshaw

CHALICE OF LIBERTY
PROTECTING RELIGIOUS FREEDOM IN AUSTRALIA

Frank Brennan – M. A. Casey – Greg Craven

CPSIA information can be obtained
at www.ICGtesting.com
Printed in the USA
BVHW041415130921
616662BV00016B/858